The Allotment Cooks A-Z Recipe Book

Dedications

I would like to dedicate this book to all of my Grandparents. All
fantastic gardeners and one phenomenal cook. Love and miss you all.
Nanny cakes forever....

Sarah Godfrey
Alan Godfrey
Ted Popkin
Winifred Wiser

Also:
My Husband Richard and our Children:-
Abigail and George.
My inspiration for life.

And finally,
Many thanks to the wonderful and inspiring Allotment Cooks for
your continued contributions.

The Allotment Cooks A-Z Recipe Book

The list of recipes in this book has been designed with growers of fruit and vegetables in mind. As we all, occasionally, have gluts of specific produce, I hope that having the main ingredient listed will enable you to find your ideal recipes quicker.

Contents:

Nanny Cakes Page 178

The Allotment Cooks A-Z Recipe Book.

Forward by Jayne Hickling.

I have always counted my blessing that I grew
up in a family of gardeners and cooks. Home
cooked food was always the normal way of
things in our house and growing food and
amazing plants and flowers was always a part
and parcel of visits to my Grandparents. I am
lucky. When most other children had shop
bought food, we always had homemade. As
such, cooking was something we always "did".
The smell of bubbling marmalade in the

kitchen and the latest jam with cellophane tops, the joining in of the
village harvest festivals and growers competitions in the old village
hall along with bike rides to forage for blackberries seems to me just
to have been part and parcel of growing up the 1970's and 1980's.
I remember the plot at the end of my Nan and Grandad's garden and
the shelling of pea pods fresh off the plant during summer holiday
visits, under the flight path of Heathrow airport, proving that you can
grow food anywhere. Runner beans, English Mustard and homemade
Curry are all things I still associate with my Nan, but not to forget
the Nanny cakes, which I claim to have named!
I loved cooking when I was at school, although I also liked
experimenting, which wasn't a part of my cookery teacher's plans. I
can still see the frustration on her face when I didn't put egg yolk in
my chocolate mousse, as demanded by the recipe! Spending time at
friend's houses after school making lasagne, whilst pretending to
present the latest cookery programme to a non- existent audience and
camera should have been an indication to a vocation! Then
university called and the need for cheap and, by then, vegetarian
food called. The things which can be created from a can of cheap
beans… who knew! It wasn't until the loss of my Grandparents that I
remembered and looked back to the growing side of food.

The first summer after we lost them, I grew my own Runner Beans, Peas and Onions for the first time. Planted a California Lilac by the kitchen window, not realising the number of bees it would draw to it and how well they would pollinate my small crop. The loss of my last Grandparent was also followed by a summer dedicated to the garden and I still use her indoor miniature watering can for my seedlings.

More time then I would like to admit has passed since then, and I have a family of my own. My hope is that home cooking and growing is as much a part of their childhood as it was for me. Inspiration is all around us. I am also fortunate to have so many people who think and feel the same, and who are willing to share their ideas and inspiration for own grown produce, using their own tried and tasted ideas in the kitchen. Some of the recipes have come from around the world, which means that some of the recipes use different measurements, but they have all come from contributors and some have their own original messages still attached. I thank them for their inspiration and hope that you find something within this book to inspire, grow and cook and maybe to create your own memories too.

A

Apples

Apple Maple Jam by Kate Wood

2.8 litres (about 2.7kg) chopped apples
1.35 kg sugar
1 teaspoon (5ml) cinnamon
½ teaspoon each allspice and nutmeg
¼ teaspoon cloves
240 ml maple syrup

Wash, core, and peel apples. Chop into 1.25cm pieces. Combine all ingredients and bring to a boil. Stir until sugar dissolves and bring to a rolling boil. Boil to 105°C and test as usual for gelling. Fill jars as usual.
Notes: I got about 8 135ml jars out of this batch. You can use any type of apple, but the consistency will be different if you use Bramleys compared to some kind of firmer apple. You'll get a more spreadable jam with Bramleys or another fluffy cooking apple, but a firmer dessert apple will give you a more pie filling sort of texture. I'd definitely go for something tart, to offset the maple syrup. This is great on ice cream and as a pie or pastry filing! Enjoy!

Apple, Sultana and Date Chutney by Jane Scrivens.

4 ½ lb cooking apples, peeled, cored and chopped finely
3 onions, peeled and chopped finely
1 inch fresh root ginger, peeled and chopped finely
4oz sultanas
4oz ready-to-eat stoned dates, chopped
1 tsp mustard seeds
1 ¾ pints cider vinegar
1lb 2oz granulated sugar

Put all the ingredients into a preserving pan and mix thoroughly. Cook on a low heat, stirring until the sugar has dissolved, then bring to the boil. Once boiling point has been reached reduce the heat and simmer gently for about 1 ½ hours. Stir continuously near the end of the cooking time so that the chutney does not catch on the base of the pan. The mixture is ready when it is thick and sticky and has reduced in volume. Pot and seal in the usual way. Keep for one month before using. Dried cranberries, figs or apricots may be used instead of dates. Brown sugar may be used instead of white. I used malt vinegar instead of cider vinegar because that was to hand in the store cupboard.

Image by Vanessa Brett Davey.

6

Apple Cake by Jean Stiff.

2 eggs
1 3/4 cups sugar
2 heaping teaspoons cinnamon
1/2 cup oil
6 medium Gala or any crisp apples
2 cups flour
2 teaspoons baking soda

Preheat oven to 180c. In a large bowl, mix the wet ingredients of eggs, sugar, cinnamon and oil. Peel and slice the apples and add to mixture in bowl (keep mixing each time you add the apples so that you stop the apples from turning brown.) Mix together the dry ingredients, baking soda and flour and add to these into the bowl. Mix well (I used a fork) until all of the flour is properly mixed in and there aren't any lumps. Pour mixture into a greased one two 9" sandwich tins or a loaf tin. Bake for approximately 55 minutes.

Spiced Apples with Rosemary- Preserve by Jacqui Bones.

1/4 pint pickling vinegar
6 tbs honey
8-10 eating apples
Springs of fresh rosemary
Optional 1tsp whole mixed spice

Put the vinegar and honey into a pan and heat gently until it boils simmer for 2 minutes peel the apples and cut into eights removing the cores. Add to the pan with the all spice simmer gently for 10 minutes or until almost transparent but not to soft
Spoon into hot jars adding 1-2 springs of rosemary to each jar seal. Store for 2-3 days before use. Makes approx 2lb

Apple and mint jelly by Vanessa Brett Davey.

1.8 kg Cooking apples
20g bunch of mint tied with string
50g mint leaves chopped finely
570ml of water
570ml White Wine Vinegar
Sugar at a ratio of 454g to 570ml
of liquid

Image by Vanessa Brett Davey, Apple and mint jelly

Prepare the apples. Don't peel or core, just chop into chunky pieces and remove any pips that have been cut as these can make the juice bitter. Jelly bag method Add the apple chunks to a large heavy bottomed saucepan. Add the bunch of mint and the pint of water. Simmer (lid on) until the apples look fluffy and are entirely soft. Strain through a jelly bag overnight. Measure the amount of apple juice and add 4/5ths of white wine vinegar (e.g. 715ml of juice would need 570ml of vinegar). Put the juice and the vinegar into a heavy bottomed saucepan. Heat gently. Add white granulated sugar 454g to 570ml of liquid and stir until you are absolutely sure that all the sugar has been dissolved. Bring to a rolling boil and test for set after 20 minutes. Testing every four minutes thereafter. If you have a jam thermometer – my jelly set at 103c. When the jelly has set, remove from the heat and stir in the chopped mint. Leave the jelly for at least 10 minutes before giving it a final stir and ladling into hot sterilised jars. Wipe the tops of the jars, seal immediately and label when cold.

The Colonel's Apple Chutney by Jacqui Bones.

1lb cooking apples peeled cored and sliced
6oz onions peeled and minced
2 cloves of garlic crushed
3/4 pint pickling vinegar
1/2 dark brown sugar
6oz raisins
2-3oz stem ginger or crystallised ginger finely chopped
1tsp salt
1 1/2 tsp dry mustard
Good pinch of cayenne pepper optional

Place the apples onions garlic and vinegar in pan bring to boil
simmer gently until soft and pulpy about 20 minutes. Add the rest of
the ingredients bring back to the boil stirring until the sugar has
dissolved. Simmer I covered until the chutney is thick with no excess
liquid on the surface stir occasionally pour into warmed jars and seal.
Store for at least a week before use makes approx 2 1/4 lb

Asparagus

Asparagus Quiche by Jayne Hickling.

4oz margarine
8oz plain flour
Water
8 eggs
12 spears of asparagus
1 large brown onion
3oz cheese
spot of milk

Make up the pastry by crumbing together the margarine and flour.
Slowly add some water until a dough is formed. Grease and flour a
baking tin and line with the pastry. Pop this in the oven for aroun 10
mins on 200c to blind bake. Next mix together the egg, milk and
grated cheese (keep some cheese back for the topping) In a pan,
brown off the onion in some oil and then add some chopped
asparagus (leaving 8 equal length spears for the top). Once the
onions are browned off, add the egg mixture and partly cook, so that
it is not quite scrambled eggs, but is still runny. Poor the partly
cooked egg mix into the pastry case and top with the remaining
asparagus spears and
cheese. Bake in the
preheated oven at 200c
for around 25 minutes,
until browned and
slightly "wobbly".

Image by Jayne Hickling. Asparagus Quiche

Asparagus and Mint Soup by Jayne Hickling.

15 large Asparagus Spears
Handful of Mint
1 Small Potato
1 Onion
Vegetable Stock (cube)
1 ½ pints boiling water.
2 Teaspoons of cooking oil.
2 teaspoons of Cornflour (optional)

Chop up all of the vegetables and shred the mint, keeping one asparagus spear to the side. In a large pan, heat the oil. Lower the heat to medium and then add the vegetables and mint. Once the vegetables have softened, but not browned, add in the vegetable stock. Cover the pan and simmer for 15 minutes. Once all of the vegetables are cooked through, blend the contents of the pan. The potato should act as a natural thickener. If the soup is not thick enough for your taste, mix the (optional) cornflower with a little water to make a paste. Add this to the soup and boil until the soup thickens. Add the remaining asparagus spear, thinly chopped, to the soup. Simmer for a final five minutes.

B
Banana

Banana Rum Jam by Bev Toogood.

2 lbs ripe bananas
3 3/4 Cup brown sugar
1 1/3 Cup water
juice of 3 limes (or lemons)
1 teaspoon cinnamon
3 tablespoons of pure vanilla extract (or use real vanilla beans, I do because I like the black speckles)
1 dash of powdered ginger
1/4 Cup of rum

Peel and mash the bananas.
Mix water, lime juice, sugar, cinnamon, vanilla, ginger over moderate heat and stir until syrup thickens. Add the mashed bananas and let cook 20 to 25 minutes, stirring occasionally. Add rum during the last few minutes of cooking to let alcohol burn off. Immediately jar and seal. Sublime on toast.

Banana Curd by Lisa Johnston.

4 Bananas
Juice of a lemon
125g butter
1 ½ cup of sugar
4 eggs.

Mash bananas and juice. Melt butter and sugar. Put 3 tablespoons of mashed banana into beaten eggs and the rest into butter and sugar and cook for ten minutes but do not boil. Add banana and eggs cook till it coats back of the spoon. You will see white cooked bits of eggs but it's fine. Makes 2 small pots.

Broad Beans

Bessara by Jayne Hickling

(Hummus style dip using beans instead of chickpeas)•
8 oz dried fava beans OR Broad Beans!!
2 cloves garlic, or to taste
80ml cup olive oil
60ml lemon juice
2 tablespoons (or more) reserved cooking liquid
1 1/2 teaspoons salt
1 tsp ground cumin
1/2 tsp sweet paprika
1/2 tsp hot paprika or cayenne pepper

Put the broad beans (or peeled fava beans) into a medium-sized pot and cover with a generous amount of water. Bring to a boil over high heat, then reduce the heat to medium and simmer the beans until are tender. This may take about an one hour or longer!! Drain the beans, but keep the liquid. Put the drained beans to a food processor, and add the garlic, olive oil, lemon juice, two tablespoons of the cooking liquid, and spices. Blitz on high speed until smooth, adding extra cooking liquid if needed to thin the bessara. Ideally it should be thin enough to pour out onto a plate, but this is down what you like. Taste the bessara and add more seasoning if you want. You can reheat the bessara and serve warm, but chilled is just as nice.

Beetroot

Beetroot Chutney- No Apples!! By Jacqui Bones.

1.8kg beetroot cooked
225g onions
450g raisins or sultanas
15g salt
225g white sugar
600ml white vinegar
6 peppercorns
6 cloves
1 tablespoon allspice

Chop the beetroot onions place the spices in muslin bag put everything in a pan bring to a slow simmer and simmer for 1-2 hours until most of the liquid has gone put into warmed jars.

Beetroot Jelly by Anne Robinson.

1lb cooked beetroot, cubed
One packet of raspberry jelly
½ pint boiling water to melt jelly
¼ pint White vinegar
2 tbsp lemon juice
Cold water to make jelly up to a pint

Pack jars with beetroot and pour jelly over.
Shake jars to ensure no air spaces and further top up if needed. Easy peasy!

Beetroot Burgers by Jayne Hickling.

These are approximate amounts, as I just threw it together and forgot
about measuring!!! (sorry!!!)
One large Beetroot
Two Carrots
One Clove of Garlic
One Onion
100ml Dried lentils, soaked in boiling water- up to 200ml (soak for
approx. 3 hours)
1 tsp Cumin
1tsp Paprika
1 Egg (optional)
Plain Flour (enough to make a firm patty!)
Cooking oil

First soak the lentils until they have re-constituted. Grate the root
vegetables, then add the dried/ reconstituted lentils. Mix in the spices
and then stir in the egg (optional if looking for a vegan recipe).
Finally mix in enough flour to be able to form burgers/ patties in
your hands (until the mixture isn't sticky, but holds together and
isn't too dry) Put a shallow amount of oil into a frying pan and
brown both sides of the burgers, then either put to the side to cool
down before bagging and freezing or cook through thoroughly- for
around 10 minutes in total - to make sure that the burger is cooked
through. If you're freezing them, reheat and cook them in a pan- they
don't re-cook well in the oven.

Beetroot and Orange Cake by Chris Murray.

200g plain flour,
¾ tsp of baking powder,
Bicarbonate soda,
Ground cinnamon,
¼ tsp salt,
½ tsp vanilla extract,
50g soft brown sugar,
125g light muscovado sugar,
3 large eggs,
300ml vegetable oil,
225g coarsely grated raw beetroot
½ zest of an orange.

Mix all the dry products together really well. Then mix all the wet together and then mix wet and dry together well. Finally add the beetroot and orange zest together. Cook for 40 minutes.

Icing; 50g unsalted butter, zest ½ orange, 125g Soft cream cheese, 100g icing sugar. Mix butter icing sugar and zest together when soft and smooth add Soft Cream Cheese and mix until smooth.

Image by Jacqui Bones, Mixed Chutneys and Preserves.

Beetroot and Apple Chutney by Jane Scrivens.

2lb raw beetroot, shredded or grated
1lb onions, skinned and chopped finely
1lb 8oz cooking apples, peeled, cored and grated
1lb seedless raisins
2 pints malt vinegar
2lb sugar
Root ginger (finger's length) chopped and tied in a muslin (I use an old clean hankie!!)

Place all the ingredients in a preserving pan and bring to the boil, making sure that all the sugar is dissolved. Simmer gently over a moderate heat, uncovered, for about an hour until soft and pulpy. Pot and cover in the usual way. It is cooked when most of the liquid is gone and it has a sticky consistency.

It is worth using a decent quality vinegar such as Sarson's for this chutney. Cheap vinegar is likely to have a harsh flavour which will overwhelm the subtle taste of the beetroot and apples. I know this from experience!

The proportion of beetroot to apple may be varied slightly according to the quantities of beetroot/apples you have, and personal taste. For my last batch I used 1 ½ lbs beetroot and 2lbs apples. (Makes about 6lb!)

Beetroot Chutney by Ann Brooks.

1kg raw beetroot.
500g onions.
750g cooking apples.
500g raisins
3tbsp ground ginger
1kg granulated sugar
1l malt vinegar

Peel and grate the beetroot. Peel and chop onions and apples. Put all ingredients in pan, bring to the boil, and then simmer until thick. Ladle into jars. Tastes best after standing for a month, but is perfectly edible before if you can't wait.

Beetroot Chutney by Jennifer Stead.

2 Cooking Apples
1 Onion
240ml Malted Vinegar
2tsp Grated Ginger
2 Whole Cloves
1tsp Ground Allspice
450g Cooked Beetroot
50g Brown Sugar
50g Raisins

Slice the apples and onions and place in the pan with the vinegar, ginger, allspice and cloves. Boil, then simmer for 20 mins. Peel and chop the beetroot, add to the pan with sugar and raisins. Boil and simmer for 15mins. Spoon into warm sterilised jars and seal. Can be eaten immediately- but best after 4 weeks.

Beetroot Relish by Heidi Whyley.

1lbs of cooking apples
1 large onion, peeled and sliced
½ tsp of ground ginger, (I always add a whole tsp)...
1 level teaspoon of salt
8 oz of soft light brown sugar
10 fluid oz malt vinegar
1 ½ lbs cooked, diced beetroot

Peel, quarter, core, and sliced the apples into a saucepan. Add the onion, sugar salt and the vinegar. Heat to dissolve the sugar and simmer for 10 - 15 minutes to cook the apple and beetroot.
Add the beetroot and cook, uncovered, until thick about an hour to an hour and a half. Great for Christmas presents!!!

Image by Nikki Mason, Mixed Chutney and Preserves.

Spicy Beetroot Soup by Lou Duggan.

5- 6 Beetroots (unskinned in a pot of water- cut off the leaves and set aside)
2x Cloves of Garlic
1 x Large Onion
2x Chilli
1x teaspoon of blackpepper
Mixed soup powder (mixed to a paste with cold water)
Root vegetable, carrots, turnips etc (the more root veg added, the thicker the soup)

Cook the beets (around 5 - 6) unskinned in a pot of water (cut off the leaves and set aside as you use them too in the soup) after 10-15 minutes boiling, the skin rubs off the beets easily under cold water. Chop them up and add back to the pot with the leaves (use the initial cooking water as the basis of the soup). Add a few cloves of garlic (I use lots), a large onion, chillies to taste/spice tolerance, teaspoon of black pepper. Mix a packet of vegetable soup in a cup of cold water and add to the pot and add any other root vegetable going, turnip, carrot to give it some bulk. Cook until all vegetables is tender and just whizz it up with a handheld blender Allow to cool then portion up and freeze. When hot crumble or grate a strong cheddar or smoked cheese in or cream/sour cream (I prefer the cheese) * Alternative- use vegetable stock cube instead of powdered soup mix. Brown off the onion, garlic and root vegetable in a little oil, before adding the liquid ingredients.

Beetroot and Horseradish Relish by Sue Imrie.

450g Beetroot. Peeled and coarsely grated.
115g Fresh Horseradish Trimmed, peeled and coarsely grated.
½ tsp Salt
115g Granulated Sugar
300ml White Wine Vinegar

Put all of the ingredients into a big bowl and stir together until the sugar dissolves. Pack into clean, dry jars and seal with a twist on lid. Label and date and keep in to fridge for up to a month.

Beetroot and Radish Stirfry by Helen Ruffles.

2 Chioggia beetroot,
Handful of radishes,
Knob of Butter and rapeseed oil
1 clove of garlic, sprig of thyme, pepper, salt, and squeeze of lemon juice.

Diced the beetroot so it is chunky. Cut handful of radishes, fry in knob of butter and rapeseed oil for about 8 minutes.
Add chopped clove of garlic, sprig of thyme, pepper, salt, and squeeze of lemon juice.
Fry for further couple of minutes.

Beetroot Chutney by Ann Brooks

1kg raw beetroot.
500g onions.
750g cooking apples.
500g raisins
3tbsp ground ginger
1kg granulated sugar
1lt malt vinegar

Peel and grate the beetroot. Peel and chop onions and Apple's.
Put all ingredient in pan, bring to the boil, then simmer until thick.
Ladle into jars. Tastes best after standing for a month, but is
perfectly edible before if you can't wait.

Beetroot Muffins by Hazel Young

10oz plain flour
1tbsp baking powder
5oz caster sugar
1tsp ground cinnamon
½ tsp ground ginger
200ml milk
2 large eggs beaten
100ml vegetable oil
3 1/2 oz beetroot grated

Preheat oven 200c and put paper cases in a 12 hole muffin tin. Mix
together sifted flour, baking powder, caster sugar, cinnamon and
ginger into a large bowl. In a separate bowl, mix all of the wet stuff
and combine milk, eggs and oil. Stir in the grated beetroot this is
where the mixture turns bright pink! Add the dry ingredients and stir
together, then spoon large dollops in to muffin tin.
Bake about 20 mins until risen and firm to touch. Leave to cool in
tin for a few minutes and then move to wire rack to cool.

Beetroot and Ginger Chutney by Jayne Hickling.

lb Beetroot, peeled, finely chopped
2lb Cooking apples, peeled, quartered, cored, roughly chopped
10oz red onions, finely chopped
1in piece fresh ginger, peeled, grated
3oz crystallised Stem Ginger, finely chopped
12oz soft light brown sugar
1 teaspoon table salt
1 teaspoon ground allspice
1 pint red wine vinegar

Peel, chop and core the beetroot, apple and red onion and put them into a large pan. Add the fresh ginger, crystallised ginger, brown sugar, salt and ground allspice. Add the vinegar and stir to mix well. Bring to the boil, then turn down the heat and simmer for about an hour, stirring every now and again, until the beetroot pieces are tender. To test to see if it is ready, spoon a little of the chutney onto a saucer. If it you can draw a line through the chutney with your finer, then it is ready to jar up. Spoon into sterilised jars and seal.

Image by Jacqui Bones.

Blackberries

Blackberry and Apple Jam by Jean Baker.

450g blackberries
450g apples
Juice of 2 large lemons (you have to use this as blackberries have no pectin)
100ml water
900g granulated sugar (not jam sugar)

Remember that apples have a lot of pectin in them already, so you don't need jam sugar- otherwise it will be really stiff!!! Put fruit, water and lemon juice in a pan and cook on a simmer for 10 minutes until fruit is softened. Put 2 small plates into the freezer to chill. Add the sugar and bring to a rolling boil. After 10 minutes put a teaspoon of mixture onto one of the plates, after a minute of it wrinkles it's ready to take off the heat, if not continue boiling for a couple more minutes. When it passes the wrinkle test I turn off the heat and let it cool for 10 minutes. Ladle the mix into sterilised jam jars and leave to set.

Blackberry and Elderberry Jam by Steven Sehmbi.

900g (2 lb) blackberries
900g (2 lb) elderberries
900g (2 lb) to 1.8kg (4 lb) jam sugar
3 to 4 tablespoons lemon juice

Wash the berries well and then drain. Remove the elderberries from their branches by stripping them off with a fork.
Put both lots of berries into a large preserving pan or large saucepan and cook over a low heat until they turn to a soft pulp. Press the berries as they cook to speed the process along and to extract as much juice as possible. If you are using very ripe berries, proceed to the next step. If the berries are still holding their shape, or are not very juicy, you can blitz them quickly in a blender at this point. Now rub the pulp through a sieve using the back of a spoon or the back of a ladle. The aim is to extract the juice and leave behind the seeds/pips. Now the very important part! Measure the resulting juice. To each 600ml of juice, add 450g of jam sugar and 1 tablespoon of lemon juice. You May not need all the sugar that you have set aside for this recipe.
Heat the juice mixture until the sugar has dissolved, then whack the heat up and boil rapidly until setting point is reached.
Ladle into hot, sterilised jars and seal. Depending on the berries, this could make anywhere between 2.5lb and 4lb of tasty jam.

Blackberry Cheese by Debs Webster.

900g (2lb) Cooking or Crab Apples
1.8kg (4lb) Blackberries
570ml (1 pint) Water
450g (1lb) Sugar per 450 g (1lb) of puree obtained

Wash, peel and chop the apples, wash and drain the blackberries and put them into a large saucepan with the water.
Bring to the boil, reduce the heat, cover and simmer until the fruit is very soft.
Squash it occasionally with the back of a wooden spoon to mix the fruit and release the juice.
Pour the mixture through a sieve over a large bowl and press through using the back of a wooden spoon.
Measure the fruit puree and allow 450g (1lb) of sugar to each 450g (1lb) of puree.
Return the puree to a clean pan, pour in the sugar and heat gently until it has dissolved.
Bring to the boil, reduce the heat and simmer until the cheese is thick.
Pour into small. Clean, dry, warm sterilised jars or moulds. Cover and seal or make into sweets. Label with contents and date when fully cool.

Sweets: Once made pour the cheese into small wide mouthed jars and treat as jam or you can use biscuit moulds to create shapes like stars and circles. You can roll into tubes or even small balls in your hands to make small treats. If you wish to dry them further, put them into a very low oven on a baking tray and then sprinkle with caster sugar. Wrap individually and pack in an airtight tin for an unusual present. You can even take it one step further and dip your dried fruit cheese sweets in chocolate. The contrast between a dark bitter high cocoa chocolate and the sweet cheese centre is sublime! Fruit cheeses are ready when you can draw a spoon across the top and leave a clean line.

Blackcurrants

Blackcurrant Jam by Jennifer Stead.

2lb Blackcurrants
1 ½ pint water
3lb Sugar (warmed)

Bring water to boil, add blackcurrants and simmer gentle for 50 minutes. Add sugar and stir until dissolved.
Bring to the boil rapidly for 10 minutes until setting point. Pour into sterilised jars immediately.

Blueberries

Blueberry and Cream Muffins by Jayne Hickling.

75g Blueberries
175ml soured cream
1/2 tsp bicarbonate of soda
1/2 teaspoon salt
175g plain flour
1/2 tsp vanilla extract
60ml vegetable oil
100g caster sugar
1 egg
Made 6 large
muffins- But you
could increase the
amount to make
more- if you have a
lot of blueberries!!

Image by Jayne Hickling, Blueberry and Cream Muffins.

Preheat the oven to 200c. Prepare number of muffin cases as required by your recipe amount. In a large bowl beat eggs and gradually add the sugar whilst beating. Continue beating while slowing pouring in the oil. Stir in the vanilla. In a separate bowl, stir together flour, salt and bicarbonate. Stir ingredients into egg mixture alternating with soured cream. Gently fold in blueberries. (the consistency reminded me of condensed milk!) Scoop/ pour the batter into the muffin cases, up to around ¾ full. Bake in the centre of a preheated oven for 25 minutes.

Blueberry, Courgette Cake by Zoe Ayling.

3 eggs, lightly beaten
1 cup vegetable oil
3 teaspoons vanilla extract
2 1/4 cups white sugar
2 cups finely shredded and drained zucchini
3 cups all-purpose flour
1 teaspoon salt
1 teaspoon baking powder
1/4 teaspoon baking soda
1 pint fresh blueberries (you can reserve a few for garnish if so desired)
Lemon Buttercream
1 cup butter, room temperature
3 1/2 cups confectioners' sugar
1 lemon, juice and zest of (about 2 tablespoons)
1 teaspoon vanilla extract
1/8 teaspoon salt

Preheat oven to 180C. Prepare two 8-inch round cake pans. Grate a large courgette (or 2 small courgettes) and place in a clean dish towel. Squeeze until most of the liquid comes out. You will want to have 2 total cups of shredded courgettes after it has been drained. Set aside.
In a large bowl and using a hand mixer, beat together the eggs, oil, vanilla, and sugar. Fold in the courgette. Slowly add in the flour, salt, baking powder, and baking soda. Gently fold in the blueberries. Divide batter evenly between prepared cake pans. Bake 35-40 minutes in the preheated oven, or until you can put in and pull out a clean skewer. Cool 20 minutes in pans, then turn out onto wire racks to cool completely.
Lemon Buttercream
Mix soft butter, sugar and salt and beat till well combined. Add lemon juice and vanilla and continue to beat for another 3 to 5 minute or until creamy. Fold in zest although if you are piping this buttercream, I recommend leaving out the zest.

Broccoli

Purple Sprouting Broccoli with Tahini by Zoe Ayling.

Purple sprouting broccoli
Tahini
Juice of 1/4 lemon
Olive oil
Black pepper
Salt (optional)

Blanche the purple sprouting broccoli and remove from pan. Heat frying pan with a tsp of olive oil.
Add a tbsp full of tahini, a squeeze of lemon juice and black pepper to taste. Stir fry for 2 minutes.
Delicious!!

Butternut Squash

Butternut Squash and Spinach Curry by Lynda Williams.

1 stalk of Lemon grass (To bruise your lemongrass, gently bash it
with the back of a knife to release its distinctive aroma.)
 1 thumb-sized piece of ginger
 1 red chilli, deseeded
 3 shallots, sliced
 3 cloves garlic, crushed
 Olive oil
 1 butternut squash, peeled and cubed
 1 400 g tin reduced fat coconut milk
 300 ml vegetable stock
 150 g baby spinach
 Small bunch fresh coriander, finely chopped
 5 ml soy sauce
 Juice of 1 lime
 1 tbsp sugar

Very finely chop the ginger, chilli, shallots and garlic and fry off in a
large pan along with the bruised lemongrass in around 5ml oil for 3-
4 minutes. Add the butternut squash and cook for a further 3-4
minutes then add the coconut milk and stock, and simmer for around
15 minutes or until the squash is tender. Add the spinach and cook
until wilted. Finish by adding finely chopped coriander, soy sauce,
the juice of a lime and the sugar. Serve with jasmine rice.

Pickled Butternut Squash with Sage and Cardamom by Linda Ford.

3 pound butternut squash, other winter squash, or pumpkin, peeled, seeded and cut into 3/4-inch cubes (about 5 cups)
1 1/2 tablespoons kosher or other coarse salt
8 whole sage leaves
1 teaspoon cardamom seeds (without pods) lightly crushed
175g cup brown sugar
425ml cups cider vinegar
175ml cup apple juice

In a non-reactive bowl, combine the squash and salt, toss to coat, and allow to stand at room temperature for about 4 hours. Drain, rinse well, and squeeze out extra moisture by the handfuls. In a medium non-reactive pot, combine all remaining ingredients and bring to a boil over medium-high heat, stirring once or twice to dissolve the brown sugar. Add the squash, bring back just to a simmer, then remove from the heat and allow to cool to room temperature, uncovered. When the mixture has cooled to room temperature, cover and refrigerate. The squash will be tasty in about 2 hours, but will improve in flavour if allowed to sit overnight. This pickle will keep, covered and refrigerated, for about 2 months.

Spicy Squash and Apple Chutney by Linda Ford.

4 tbsp vegetable oil
2 large onions, chopped
500g Bramley apples peeled and cut into ½ cubes
100g piece of ginger, peeled and thinly shredded
1 red chilli, deseeded and finely chopped
15 cardamom pods bashed open
2 long cinnamon sticks snapped in half
1 tbsp black mustard seeds
2 tsp cumin seeds
1 tsp ground turmeric
500g light soft brown sugar
325ml cider vinegar

Heat the oil and fry the onion, ginger, chilli, cardamom, cinnamon, mustard and cumin for 5 minutes. Stir in the garlic, squash and apples and cook for 10-15 minutes. Stir in the turmeric and sugar, simmer for 5 minutes. Pour in the vinegar and add the salt. Simmer for 30 minutes then pot up as usual.

Image by Alma Crosby, Squashes.

Squash, Apricot & Almond Chutney by Linda Ford.

1 small butternut squash about 800g (other squashes can be used)
400g golden granulated sugar (think I may have used Demerara sugar)
2 onions, chopped
600ml cider vinegar
225g ready to eat dried apricots, quartered
finely grated rind and juice of one orange
½ tsp turmeric
1 tbsp coriander seeds
1 tbsp salt (this can be reduced if this amount is cause for concern)
115g flaked almonds

Peel, deseed squash and cut into 2cm cubes
Put sugar and vinegar into a preserving pan and heat gently until dissolved (needs to be stirred frequently)
Add everything else except the almonds and bring to the boil slowly
Reduce the heat and simmer for 45-50 minutes
Stir frequently towards the end of the cooking time until mixture is thick consistency and no extra liquid remains
Stir in the almonds
Pot up and store in a cool, dark place. Allow at least a month before eating; consume within 2 years
Once opened keep refrigerated and eat within 2 months.

Butternut Squash Soup by Lou Duggan.

Cold water
Squash- Pumpkin etc
Root- Carrots, Parsnips, Turnips (the more root vegetable you add, the thicker the soup)
Garlic- couple of cloves
1 x Large onion
2x Fresh chilli (can use powdered/ dry)
Packet of vegetable soup

Add all the vegetables in and cook until tender then season with a lot of black pepper. If you like you can season with herbs but I think it can over power the flavour. Allow to cool slightly the blitz with a stick blender until smooth, Freeze for use during cold dark winter days, it's a very warming hearty soup. Drizzle in some cream when serving for extra richness.

Alternative- rather than using Lou's suggested packet of vegetable soup, you can just use a Vegetable Stock cube, dissolve in boiling water and put to the side. Brown off the onions in a little oil and add

the chopped vegetables. Then you can add the stock and boil until the root vegetables are soft enough to blitz.

*Image by Elaine Kelleher,
Carrot and Coriander Soup.*

C
Carrots

Carrots, Feta and Walnuts by Stephen Baird.

700g carrots, peeled and cut in half lengthways
1/2 a block of feta
1 tsp cumin seeds, dry fried and ground fresh
2 tbsp walnuts, chopped roughly and dry fried
Palm-full of fresh oregano

Toss the carrots in a couple of tbsp of olive oil and roast for 50 minutes in a fan oven at 190C (not sure of conversion temperatures) When you bring them out they should be slightly caramelised around the edges, roughly mash. Add cumin, walnuts, feta and oregano over the top and serve. We usually serve with couscous that has been dry fried with some fried onions.

Carrot and Coriander Soup by Elaine Kelleher.

2 Sliced onions
2lbs sliced carrots
A couple of handfuls of fresh coriander
2 pints vegetable stock.
1 tablespoon coconut oil (or any other oil)

Stir fry onions & carrots for a few minutes in oil. Add stock. Simmer until tender. I used a hand blender for a smooth soup or you can leave it chunky. Enjoy. Sprinkle with a little chopped coriander.

Carrot and Ginger loaf by Jacqui Bones.

4oz unsalted butter plus extra for tin
4oz dark muscovado sugar
4oz golden treacle
zest of one orange
zest and juice of one lemon
1 large carrot grated 5oz
5 balls stem ginger finely chopped
6oz self raising flour
¼ tsp bicarbonate of soda
2tsp ground ginger
¼ tsp ground black pepper
2 eggs
5oz icing sugar

Heat the oven to around 180c. Butter and line a loaf tin. Put the butter, sugar, treacle and half of the zests into a large pan heat gently until everything has melted. Add the carrot, ¾ of the chopped ginger, all of the flour, the bicarbonate, ¼ tsp salt, the ground ginger, pepper and eggs into the pan stir well until you have a smooth batter. Pour into the tin and bake for 45 minutes or until a skewer comes out clean. Cool in the tin then on a wire rack
Sift the icing sugar add the remaining zests and enough lemon juice (about 4tsp) to make a smooth thick icing cover the cake when completely cool scatter the reserved ginger on top.

This cake gets better with age, and the icing could be added two or three days after baking.

Popping Carrot Salad by Helen Ruffles.

250 g grated carrots
pinch of salt
Juice of half a lemon
Glug of oil...
1/2 tbs Mustard Seeds
1 tbs Nigella seeds (black onion seeds)

Grate carrots, add salt and lemon juice. Heat oil and fry seeds until pop. Cool and mix together. Tastes 'groovy'!!!

Brandied Carrots by Jennifer Stead.

1kg Carrots
900ml water
675g Sugar
Zest and Juice of 2 Lemons
3tsps Grated Ginger
1 ½ tbsp Brandy

Chop the carrots and put them in the pan with water and boil. Simmer for 20 minutes until very soft. Puree through a sieve and return to the pan. You could blitz them in a processor- but it won't be as smooth. Add sugar, lemon and ginger. Warm until the sugar has dissolved then boil rapidly for 15-20 minutes- until setting point. Add brandy and put into jars.

Carrot Cake by Jayne Hickling.

150g butter, melted, plus extra for greasing
75g soft light brown sugar
75g caster sugar3 free-range eggs
200g self-raising flour
1 tsp bicarbonate of soda
½ tsp salt
2 tsp ground cinnamon
½ tsp grated nutmeg
Zest of 1 orange
300g carrots, peeled and grated
100g finely chopped walnuts
For the icing:
150g full-fat cream cheese
50g light brown soft sugar
Zest of ½ lemon and a squeeze of juice

Preheat the oven to 180C and grease and line the bases of 2 x 18cm sandwich tins. Put the melted butter, sugar and eggs into a large mixing bowl and whisk well until the ingredients are thoroughly combined and the mixture has almost doubled in volume. Sift together the flour, bicarbonate, salt and spices and then fold very gently into the liquid mixture, being careful to knock as little air out as possible. Fold in the remaining ingredients and divide between the tins. Bake for about 30 minutes until a skewer inserted into the middle comes out clean. Cool in the tins. Meanwhile, beat together the icing ingredients and refrigerate. When the cakes are cool enough to ice, remove from the tins, top one with half the icing, and then the other cake. Ice the top and decorate as required.

Cauliflower.

<u>Piccalilli by Linda Ford.</u>

1 cauliflower
3 large onions
8 large shallots
1 cucumber
600ml white wine or cider vinegar
300ml white malt vinegar
1 tsp chopped dried red chilli
250g caster sugar
50g English mustard powder
25g ground turmeric
3 tbsp cornflour
salt and pepper

Cut the cauliflower into small florets, and chop the onions and shallots into 1cm dice. Gary Rhodes then salts these and leaves them to stand for 24 hours, before rinsing and drying them. I have done that in the past, but I've found little difference in the result if I skip that step. Peel and de-seed the cucumber, and cut into 1cm dice. Sprinkle with a little salt and leave for a quarter of an hour. Rinse and dry, then add to the other vegetables. Put the vinegars into a pan, together with the chilli and bring to the boil. Take off the heat and leave to stand for thirty minutes, and then strain and discard the chilli. When the vinegar is cool, mix all the dry ingredients in a bowl and add a little of the vinegar and mix until you have a thin paste. Bring the rest of the vinegar back to the boil and pour it into the sugar/spice paste and stir well. Stir well until well mixed together with no lumps. Return to the pan and simmer for about three minutes. Pour over the vegetables and mix well. Stored in sterilised jars in a cool place, this should easily keep for a month or two.

Cauliflower and Cheese Bake by Christina Mell.

4 Large Potatoes
1 full head of Cauliflower
4-6 rashers of bacon
1/2 block of mature cheddar
1 heaped dessert spoon of flour
1/2 tsp Paprika
1/2 Pint of Milk

Peel and chop up spuds. Microwave for 15 minutes (don't add water). Put in a large lasagne type dish along with a full head of cauliflower also chopped into bite-sized pieces. Cut up rashers of bacon and sprinkle over. Now, in a saucepan, grate all of the cheese. Stir in the spoon of flour and the paprika. Add a splash of milk and heat. Keep stirring and adding milk (about 1/2 pint) until its bubbling nicely and the thickness of cheese sauce. Pour the cheese sauce over the spuds, bacon and cauliflower and bake at 200c for 20-30 minutes. Serve with steamed cauliflower greens.

Pickled Cauliflower by Jacqui Bones.

2 medium cauliflowers
4 ½ salt
1 ½ pint cold water
1 ½ pint pickling vinegar

Optional
1 cinnamon stick
4 blades of mace

Cut cauliflower in to small florets put in a bowl make a brine using water and salt and pour over cauliflower weight down with a plate to keep submerged leave for 24 hours drain off and rinse well. Pack in to clean jars adding a piece of cinnamon stick and 2 blades of mace in each jar. Pour the cold vinegar in to the jars, cover completely leave for 4-6 weeks.

Cauliflower Curry by Cara Kussan.

1x Cauliflower
Curry Powder
Salt
Chilli Flakes
Chicken (or Quorn)
Peas

In a pan add one whole cauliflower chopped than add enough water to cover. Sprinkle in as much curry powder as you want any flavour salt and chill flakes. When cooked blend than add cooked chicken (or Quorn) and cooked peas.

Image by Cara Kussan, Cauliflower Curry.

Chillies

Preserved Chillies by Jacqui Bones.

250g medium-sized green and red chillies
2 bay leaves
6 black and 6 pink peppercorns
1tbsp coriander seeds
1 level tbsp salt
4 level tbsp caster sugar
600ml white wine vinegar or rice vinegar
1-2 tall jars

With a very sharp knife, cut the stalk end off the chilli and carefully slit each chilli from the stalk to the tip and remove the seeds, use the handle of a teaspoon. (Check the chillies will fit in your jar/s and trim them if necessary.) Lay the chillies down in one layer in a shallow dish, with the bay leaves, and pour boiling water over them. Leave for 5 minutes. Drain well.
Divide the peppercorns, coriander seeds and salt in the jar(s), then pack in the chillies and bay leaves.
Heat the sugar and vinegar over a low heat until the sugar dissolves. When hot, but not boiling, pour the syrup into the jar(s). Cool, put the lid(s) on. Seal and label. Chill. Leave for 2 weeks before using.

Image by Mandy Bellis, Chilli Jam and Chilli Oil.

Chilli Jam by Steven Sehmbi.

150 grams long fresh red chilli peppers (deseeded and cut into 4 pieces)
150 grams red peppers (cored, deseeded and cut into rough chunks)
1 kilogram jam sugar
600 ml cider vinegar

You will need 6 x 250ml / 1 cup sealable jars, with vinegar-proof lids, such as Kilner jars or re-usable pickle jars.
Sterilize your jars and leave to cool. Put the cut-up chillies into a food processor and pulse until they are finely chopped. Add the chunks of red pepper and pulse again until you have a vibrantly red-flecked processor bowl. Dissolve the sugar in the vinegar in a wide, medium-sized pan over a low heat without stirring.
Scrape the chilli-pepper mixture out of the bowl and add to the pan. Bring the pan to the boil, then leave it at a rollicking boil for 10 minutes. Take the pan off the heat and allow it cool. The liquid will become more syrupy, then from syrup to viscous and from viscous to jelly-like as it cools. After about 40 minutes, or once the red flecks are more or less evenly dispersed in the jelly (as the liquid firms up, the hints of chilli and pepper start being suspended in it rather than floating on it), ladle into your jars. If you want to stir gently at this stage, it will do no harm. Then seal tightly.

Chilli Jelly by Helen Ruffles.

1 1/2 lb Sour Cooking Apples with skin on roughly chopped
Approximately 1 ½ lb Granulated Sugar
Juice of 1 Lemon
1-2 tsp chilli flakes (depending on how hot you like it)
(Also need Jelly bag or Muslin)

Put the chopped apples, including the cores and pips, in a preserving pan or a large heavy based saucepan. Pour in 1.7 litres (3 pints) of cold water, bring to the boil, and simmer for 30-40 minutes or until the apples are mushy and completely stewed down. Mash them a little with a potato masher or a fork.

Spoon the pulpy mixture into a jelly bag or muslin-lined sieve set over a large clean bowl. Leave the juice to drip through naturally overnight. Don't be tempted to squeeze the pulp mixture if you want a crystal-clear jelly. Measure the strained juice and calculate 450g (1lb) of sugar for every 600ml (1 pint) of juice. (You should have around1.7litres/ 3 pints of juice). Pour the juice into a clean pan, bring to the boil, then add the sugar and lemon juice. Stir until the sugar has dissolved, then bring to a rolling boil and remove any scum that comes to the surface. Continue to boil, stirring occasionally, for 20-30 minutes or until the jelly reaches the setting point. Remove the pan from the heat while you test for a set.

Courgettes

Courgette Soup by Lesley Peachey.

500g Potatoes
1kg courgettes
Spring onions (or leek thinnings)
100 g cheddar grated cheese
pinch nutmeg and pepper

Put in potatoes and just cover with stock - cook 10 minutes. Add all of the courgette and cook for around 10 minutes. Add a handful of spring onions (or leek thinnings!) - cook 10 minutes. When all is soft blend with a hand blender then add all of the grated cheddar, a teaspoon or so grated nutmeg and plenty of pepper. Stir to mix and melt the cheese. Here I've topped it with some crispy bacon. Easy, tasty and freezes beautifully ... And uses up quite a bit of courgette!

Courgette Soup by Patricia Serrell.

Onions
Butter
1 Tbsp Cumin
1 teaspoon turmeric
Chopped Courgettes
Half Pint Veg or chicken stock
Skimmed Milk

Fry onions until slightly caramelised add some butter and a tablespoon of ground cumin and teaspoon of turmeric gently fry for a minute then masses of chopped courgette fry stirring for a few minutes to incorporate then add half pint vegetable or chicken stock and then as much skimmed milk so as to get to soup consistency bring to boil simmer 10 minutes then blitz.

Courgette Soup by Cara Kussan.

3 x Courgettes
Onions
1x Potato
Salt
Black Pepper
Cumin Seeds
Olive Oil
Water

Fry and slice onions, until soft. Add 3 chopped courgettes and one potato. Add salt, black pepper. A few cumin seeds a bit of olive oil. Water to cover. When cooked blend.

Courgette Pickle by Alison Fisher.

500ml cider vinegar
120g sugar
1 ½ tsp dry mustard
1 ½ tsp crushed yellow & brown mustard seed
1 tsp ground turmeric
500g courgettes
2tbsp salt
1 small onion

Slice courgettes and onion very thinly into discs (easier with a mandolin!) Place in bowl, add salt & mix well. Cover with very cold water & stir to dissolve salt. After 1hr drain & dry thoroughly, either in salad spinner or between towels. Combine pickling mix in saucepan & simmer for 3 minutes. Set aside until just warm. Mix courgettes & onion with the cooled liquid, transfer to sterilised jars. Cover & refrigerate for at least a day before eating. Will keep indefinitely in fridge.

Courgette all'uovo by Ieva Knell.

4 courgettes, cut into small cubes
1 onion, finely chopped
2 tbsp olive oil
100g parmesan cheese, grated
6 eggs
3 cloves garlic (optional)
salt and pepper to taste
bread to serve with

Fry onion and courgettes in a frying pan with olive oil. While they are softening and turning golden brown, beat the eggs, Parmesan and salt and pepper together. Once the courgettes and onions are tender, add the egg mixture to the pan and make a scrambled egg consistency. Serve with bread or to accompany a mail meal. My variation: I added a handful of parboiled green beans to the courgettes since I grew up making this dish with green beans from the allotment instead of courgettes. And I added about 3 cloves of garlic, sliced, before the eggs went in. I'm a bit of a garlic nut and put it into most of the savoury recipes.

Image by Lesley Peachey. Courgette Soup, Courgette Bread and Red Currant Jelly.

Courgette and Orange Cake by Alison Fisher.

350g finely grated courgette (I don't bother peeling)
200g soft brown sugar,
125ml veg oil ,
3 eggs ,
1sp vanilla essence,
100g sultanas or raisins (but I imagine most dried fruit would go well.)
300g self raising flour
1 tsp baking powder,
zest of one orange.

Finely grate courgettes and squeeze out excess water. You then mix with oil, eggs, orange zest, vanilla and dried fruit. Get the flour and fold it in with the baking powder, but don't over mix it!!! Bake about 45-50 minutes on gas mark 4.

For frosting: 200g Philadelphia soft cheese and 100g icing sugar plus a bit more orange zest mix together and chill whilst cake baking.

Courgette and Cheese Loaf by Brian Sturrock.

75g Butter
200g Courgettes (weighed topped and tailed)
225g Self raising four
¼ tsp salt
¼ tsp Cayenne Powder
½ tsp dry mustard powder
125g Grated Mature Cheddar Cheese
3 Large Eggs
4 tbsp Milk

Preheat oven to 180c. Line a 2lb loaf tin with baking paper. Melt the butter and leave to cool.- don't allow to solidify. Grate the courgettes and set aside, sift the flour, salt, cayenne powder and mustard powder into a bowl. Stir in the cheese. Lightly beat the egg, milk and melted butter together with a fork. Add to the flour along with the courgettes and stir until just evenly mixed. Put the mixture in the loaf tin and level the top. Bake for 45-50 minutes or until the top springs back when lightly pressed. Cool on a wire rack.

Image by Naomi Pickard,
Courgette and Cheese Loaf and
Ratatouille.

Lemon and Courgette Cake by Alice Duckworth.

200g Grated Courgette
150g Caster Sugar
1 Egg
125ml Vegetable Oil
200g Plain Flour
½ tsp Salt
2 tsp Lemon Zest
½ tsp Bicarbonate of Soda
¼ tsp Baking Powder
1tsp Cinnamon

Preheat the oven to 160c (fan) Grease a loaf tin. In a bowl, beat together courgette, sugar, eggs and oil. In another bowl, sift together flour, salt, bicarbonate of soda and baking powder. Stir in cinnamon and lemon zest. Stir the flour mixture into batter until just blended. Pour into the tin. Bake for 45 minutes. Cool for 10 minutes before turning out.

Courgette, Potato and Feta Bake by Pauline Lord.

4 medium sized potatoes (about 600g), peeled
Half a bunch of spring onions (about 4- or 1 medium onion, peeled
and finely sliced
2 medium to large courgettes (salted if large)
200g feta cheese
4 sprigs of mint
2 tbsp olive oil
300ml vegetable stock made with 1 rounded tsp vegetable Bouillon
powder or ½ a vegetable stock cube
Freshly ground black pepper

Preheat the oven to 190°C/375°F/Gas 5. Trim the roots and the top
half of the green leaves off the spring onions. Cut them lengthways
into quarters then across into three. Halve and finely slice the
potatoes. Cut the ends off each courgette and slice the rest finely.
Pull the leaves off the mint and chop roughly. Pour 1 tbsp of olive oil
into a large baking dish and smear it round the base and sides of the
dish. Put a layer of potatoes over the bottom of the dish (about one
third of the sliced potato) top with half the onions, half the sliced
courgettes and half the feta, evenly crumbled over the courgettes.
Scatter over half the mint and season with freshly ground black
pepper. Repeat with another layer of potato, onion, courgette, feta
and mint then finish with a layer of potato. Pour the stock over the
vegetables then trickle the remaining olive oil over the top of the
dish. Bake for an hour to an hour and a quarter or until the potatoes
are completely tender (you should be able to stick a knife through
them easily) and the top is brown and crispy. (About half way
through the cooking time tilt the pan and spoon a little of the juices
over the potatoes.) Nice on its own but even better with a tomato
salad.

Courgette Marmalade by Mary Fothergill.

1 Kilo Courgettes
1 Kilo Caster Sugar
3 Lemons and zest
1 inch Ginger

Put all of the ingredients into a pan. Mix together over a low heat until the sugar dissolves. Increase the heat. Let it bubble and skim off any scum.Cool some on a small plate to test the set. When marmalade looks thick it is nearly ready. You can also drag a spoon along the pan and see if the mix stays separated. Add extra lemon zest / ginger. Pour into jars.

Courgette Chutney by Ben Farrier.

1kg Courgette
1 Tart Apple, Peeled and cored
1 Medium Onion
1 Green Pepper
1 Garlic Clove, Minced
250g Dark Brown Sugar
250ml White Wine Vinegar
1 Tablespoon Grated Fresh Root Ginger
1 Tablespoon English Mustard
¼ Teaspoon Crushed Red Chilli Flakes
½ Teaspoon Salt

Peel courgette and discard and large seeds, chop into small pieces. Finely chop apple, onion and green pepper; place in a casserole along with courgette and remaining ingredients. Bring to the boil. Reduce heat and simmer, uncovered, over a medium heat until thick, about 45 to 55 minutes, stirring often. Cool. Ladle into jars and refrigerate.

Courgette Pakora by Ham Yam.

1 large courgette/2 small, grated
A good sprinkle of salt
1/2 sliced onion (optional)
Chopped red chilli (optional)
1 tsp curry powder/garam masala
1 tsp salt
1 tsp bicarb/baking powder
About 1/2 mug of Gram flour (plain flour would be fine!)

Grate a large courgette into a sieve, sprinkle in salt and leave for at least an hour to drain of moisture.
Add all the other ingredients into a bowl with the courgette, using enough flour to bind the mixture til it's sticky and holds together enough to fry. Fry in plenty of oil until brown, crispy and delicious!

Pickled Courgettes/ Marrow by Tracey Colley.

500g Courgettes/marrow
2 Red Onions
Finely sliced Red chilli - to suit personal taste
3tbsp Salt

Slice vegetables, sprinkle with salt, cover with cold water and leave for an hour. Drain thoroughly and pat dry with kitchen paper. Meanwhile, put;

500ml cider vinegar
140g sugar
1tsp mustard powder
1 tsp mustard seeds
1tsp celery seeds
1tsp chilli flakes and 1tsp turmeric
In a pan and bring to a simmer. Simmer for about 3 minutes, till sugar dissolved. Leave to cool till warm, but not hot. Pack vegetables into jars and cover with warm vinegar and seal. I usually leave for at least a week (if temptation doesn't get the better of me) to mature.

Image by Karen Synnuck, Chocolate Courgette cake, Cheese and Courgette Scones.

Cheese and Courgette Scones by Alice Duckworth.

450g Self Raising Flour
112g Margarine
340g Courgette (skin on and grated)
112g Grated Cheddar
14 tbsp Milk
1 Tbsp Salt
2 Level tsp Baking Powder
1 Level tsp Mustard Powder

Preheat oven to 200c (fan oven). Grate courgettes and place in a bowl with salt and leave for 10 minutes. Sift flour and baking powder into a bowl then rub in margarine until it resembles fine breadcrumbs. Return to Courgettes. Place in a clean tea towel and squeeze out moisture and then add to the breadcrumb mixture and mix in. Add cheese and mustard powder and stir in. Finally slowly add the milk to make a soft manageable dough (you may not need all of the liquid). Tip onto a floured worktop and roll out to 2.5 cm deep. Cut into rounds using 3 inch Pastry cutter. Should make 8 big scones. Top each scone with grated cheese and place on a greased baking tray. Bake for 18-20 minutes.

Courgette Fries by Helen Ruffles.

2 Courgettes
1 egg white
1/4 cup milk
1/2 cup shredded Parmesan cheese
1/2 cup seasoned breadcrumbs
Organic olive oil

Preheat oven to 220C. Cut courgettes into 3-inch sticks. Whisk an egg white in a small bowl, and add milk. Combine Parmesan and seasoned breadcrumbs in a separate bowl. Dip courgette sticks into egg mixture, and then roll in breadcrumb mixture. Coat a baking sheet with olive oil, and place courgettes on sheet. Bake for 25–30 minutes or until golden brown. As a suggested alteration- use Polenta instead of breadcrumbs???

Image by Ali Fisher, Pickled Courgettes.

Sweet Pickled Gherkins by Helen Hunter.

5-6 Gherkins or 3 cucumbers or 3 courgettes
1 Large Onion
25g Salt
300ml Cider vinegar (Or Distilled White Vinegar)
225g Sugar
½ Level tsp ground turmeric
¼ Level tsp ground cloves
1 Tbsp Mustard Seeds

Thinly slice gherkins. Peel and thinly slice onions
Arrange in layers in a mixing bowl, sprinkling salt between each
layer. Cover with a weighted plate and leave for 3 hours.
After this the gherkins and onions will be swimming in water. Pour
this away and thoroughly rinse and drain the vegetables.
Put vinegar, sugar and spices into a saucepan. The tumeric will turn
the pickle bright green. Stir over low heat till sugar has dissolved.
Add gherkins and onion. Bring to the boil and boil for 1 minute only
- vegetables will remain crisp and draw off the heat. Using a
perforated spoon transfer gherkins, onion and mustard seed to
storage jars. Return the pan to the heat and boil rapidly for 10
minutes to reduce the liquid and concentrate the flavours. Pour this
syrup over the vegetables in the jars. Cover tightly when cold.

Pickled Peppers and Courgettes by Linda Ford.

2 large red peppers
2 medium-sized red chillies, deseeded and thinly sliced
1½ oz (40 g) sea salt, lightly crushed
2 lb 8 oz (1.15 kg) courgettes (no need to peel)
12 oz (350 g) red onion (about 3 onions), peeled
1½ pints (850 ml) good-quality white wine vinegar
8 oz (225 g) Demerara sugar1 oz
(25 g) mustard seeds
1 teaspoon celery seeds
1 rounded teaspoon ground turmeric
½ teaspoon ground mace
You will also need four 17½ fl oz (500 ml) preserving jars, sterilised.

Start this the night before. First, deseed the peppers, cut out any pith and slice them into 2 inch (5 cm) strips. Next, trim and slice the courgettes into diagonal ½ inch (1 cm) slices. After that, halve the onions and cut them into 1/4 inch (5 mm) slices Now pack the vegetables into a large colander in layers, sprinkling each layer with salt, put a dish underneath it to catch the juices and another with a weight on top, and leave them overnight. Next day, rinse the vegetables under cold, running water, really press them to get rid of any excess moisture, and pat them dry with a clean tea cloth. Then leave them spread out on the cloth for about 2 hours to thoroughly dry off. After that, place the vinegar, sugar and spices, including the chillies, in a saucepan and stir them together over a medium heat until the sugar has completely dissolved. Let it all simmer for about 3 minutes and then add the vegetables, simmering for another 3 minutes. Then divide the pickle between the hot, sterilised jars (see below), packing it right up to the top. Swivel them to make sure the air is expelled and really press the vegetables down under the liquid before you place waxed discs on top. Then seal tightly with vinegar-proof lids, label the jars when cold and store the pickles in a cool, dry, dark place. They are supposed to be kept for 3 months to mellow before eating (if you are patient), but I've found them to be very good in about a month. To sterilise jars: wash the jars and lids in warm, soapy water, rinse well (again in warm water), then dry them thoroughly with a clean tea cloth, place them on a baking tray and pop them in a medium oven, 180°C for a minimum of 5 minutes. Add their contents while they are still hot.

Cranberries

Cranberry Chutney by Jayne Hickling.

2 tbsp vegetable oil
1 red onion, finely chopped
1 chilli, finely chopped
200g Demerara sugar
150ml cider vinegar
250g fresh cranberries
100g dried apricots
salt and freshly ground black pepper
1 tsp ground cloves

Heat the oil in large saucepan and fry the onion and chilli for 4-5 minutes, or until softened. Add the sugar, vinegar, cranberries, seasoning and cloves. Bring the mixture to the boil and cook for a further 15 minutes, or until the mixture has thickened when you run a spoon through it.

Cucumbers

Cucumber Relish from Auntie Win from NZ./ Nan Roberts Massey

1 lb apples, peeled,
1 Large Onion
2 large cucumbers,
1 lb white sugar,
1 pint wine vinegar,
1 teaspoon pepper,
1oz salt.

Mince apples and cook in vinegar until soft, add onions minced, sugar salt and pepper, cook till soft then add minced cucumber boil for five minutes and seal in jars. I remember this being amazing on ham. Suggested addition- boil the mix until it thickens to a chutney consistency.

Cucumber Pickle (1) by Jacqui Bones.

1 1/2 cucumbers
1/2 lb onions peeled and thinly sliced
2 level tablespoons of salt
1/2 pint pickling vinegar
5oz caster sugar
1 level teaspoon dill seed

Thinly slice the cucumber place in large bowl with the onions sprinkle with salt leave to stand for about 1 hour rinse well and drain very well. Put the vinegar in a pan itch the sugar and dill seed heat gently until the sugar has dissolved then bring to a boil and boil for 3 minutes. Pack the cucumber and onions in clean jars pour the vinegar into the jars to cover the contents seal at once store for 2-3 weeks. Makes 2 1/2lb

Cucumber Pickle 2 by Jacqui Bones.

1.5 kg cucumber, sliced very thinly, using a mandolin if possible (I put gherkins in as not enough cucumbers).
700 g onions, halved and sliced very thinly, using a mandolin if possible
80 g sea salt
500 ml cider vinegar
350 g granulated sugar
4 tsp mustard seeds
a few whole cloves
½ tsp ground turmeric

Layer the cucumber and onion in a colander over a bowl, sprinkling with the sea salt as you go. Weigh them down with a plate and leave for a few hours. Rinse the vegetables well to get rid of the salt and drain off the liquid in a colander. Combine the vinegar, sugar, mustard seeds, cloves and turmeric and mix in a pan. Bring slowly to the boil, stirring until the sugar has completely dissolved. Add the well-drained cucumber and onion mixture and bring back to the boil for 1 minute. You may need to do this in several batches if you don't have a big preserving pan. Mix well so the spices are evenly distributed and using a slotted spoon, transfer the mixture to sterilised jars, leaving the liquid in the pan. Bring the liquid back to the boil and simmer until slightly reduced for about 15 minutes, then divide it between the 6 cucumber-filled jars, filling them to the brim. Put on the lids and label jars with the contents and date. The cucumbers will be ready to eat after 4-6 weeks. Store in a cool dark place and use within 12 months, put in fridge after opening and eat within 3 months. Don't be surprised if you end up with more than fits in 6 jars, any leftovers can be kept in the fridge to be eaten over the next few days. A little word of warning about turmeric- this spice easily stains skin, plastic and clothing so keep it away from all three.

Sweet Cucumber Relish by Teresa Witham.

Sweet Cucumber Relish
1kg800g cups chopped unpeeled cucumbers
750g chopped bell pepper
150g chopped celery
150g chopped peeled onion
½ cup salt
1 ½ pint white vinegar
500g cups granulated sugar
4 tablespoons mustard seeds
2 tablespoons celery seeds (optional)

Put chopped vegetables in a large bowl. Stir in the salt, cover, and let stand at room temperature for 4 hours. Put the vegetables in a large colander and drain. Rinse with cold water. In a large pan, combine the vinegar, sugar, mustard seeds, and celery seeds. Bring to a boil over medium-high heat. Add the drained vegetables and stir to blend. Bring back to a full boil; reduce heat to medium-low and simmer for 15 minutes. Fill warm sterilised jars and seal immediately.
Depending on your preference roughly or finely chop vegetables.

Cucumber and Onion Raita by Jayne Hickling.

1 Cucumber, peeled and cubed
1 Small Onion, Cut into rings
1 tsp Salt
1 tsp Lime Juice
1 tsp Honey
¼ pint (150 ml) Natural, Plain Yoghurt

Sprinkle the cucumber and onion with salt and leave to drain for 15 minutes. Place in a bowl. Beat together the remaining ingredients, fold into the cucumber and onion and chill for 15 minutes before serving. Can keep in the fridge for a couple of days.

Image by Nan Massey Roberts, Cucumber Relish.

D
Damsons

Damson Jam by Jackie Peat.

5lb Damsons
6lb Granulated Sugar
1 Pint Water

Put the fruit into the preserve pan with the water and bring to the boil, then reduce to simmer until it has reduced by 1/4. Count the number of Damsons you put into the pan. Then leave to cool. Once cooled remove the stones. Count the stones as you remove them to make sure that you remove the amount of stones for the amount of plums put into the pot!! Then bring back up on the heat and add the sugar, stirring in well. Keep boiling until it reaches setting point and then put into sterilised jars.

Image by Vanessa Brett Davey, Damsons.

Dried Mixed Fruit

Nain's Fruit Loaf by Nan Roberts Massey.

Been using mother grandmother recipe for years..
10 oz of dried mixed fruit
2 mugs hot tea
1 pot of glace cherries.
3 oz brown sugar
1 egg
12 oz S/R flour.
A good heaped teaspoon if mixed spice.

Put the 10oz of dried mixed fruit into two mugs and soak in hot tea overnight with a pot of glace cherries. Next day add 3 oz brown sugar an egg and 12 oz Sr flour. A good heaped teaspoon if mixed spice. In a 1 lb loaf tin cook till cooked on 160, usually an hour.

Fruit Loaf Cake by Helen Ruffles.

3oz Cubed Margarine
3oz white or brown sugar
2-4oz mixed dried fruit, coconut or chocolate chips, nuts, glace cherries or whatever is in the cupboard!!
8fl oz milk
12oz Self Raising Flour
1 egg

Mix margarine, sugar, mixed fruit and "bits" together and add the milk. Mix in the dried ingredients, alternating between them and the beaten egg. Spoon in to a 1lb loaf tin. Bake in the middle of an oven at 170 for around 1 hour, until an inserted skewer comes out clean!!!

Bread Pudding by Jane Scrivens.

1 small loaf of bread – about 14oz
4oz sugar – any kind
6oz grated suet, butter or margarine
5tsp mixed spice
1lb mixed dried fruit
1tbsp marmalade
2 eggs, beaten

Break up the bread, place in a bowl and cover with milk and water. Leave to stand for 30 minutes. You can place a plate ontop to weigh down the bread and make sure it stays in the fluid. Tip any excess liquid away. Add suet, sugar, spice, dried fruit, marmalade and eggs. Stir well. The consistency should be soft and dropping, like cake mixture. If too dry add a little milk . Pour into a greased roasting tin and bake for 1 hour at 160 degrees, then ½ hour at 180 degrees.

Image by Jane Scrivens. Christmas Pudding.

Christmas Pudding by Jane Scrivens.

1lb stoned or seedless raisins
12oz sultanas
12oz currants
4oz chopped candied peel
2oz flaked blanched almonds
2oz plain flour
2 teaspoons mixed spice
1 teaspoon powdered cinnamon½ teaspoon grated nutmeg
8oz soft brown sugar
8oz fresh wholemeal breadcrumbs
Grated rind of 1 lemon
4oz shredded suet
4 eggs
½ bottle brown ale
¼ pint whisky

Mix together all the raisins, sultanas, currants and peel in a mixing bowl. Pour the beer over the mixture, cover with a plate or cling film and leave overnight. The next day, tip the fruit mixture into a very large mixing bowl. Sieve the flour and spices together and add to the fruit mixture with the sugar, breadcrumbs and suet. Beat the eggs into the mixture with the whisky. Stir well and wish. Leave the mixture overnight to stand, covered with a large plate. The next day divide the mixture between the greased pudding basins; either one 4 pint, two 2 pint or four 1 pint basins. Press the mixture in firmly. Cover with a circle of greaseproof paper and the foil tied on with string. Steam for 4-8 hours depending on size; the larger the pudding the longer the cooking time. Allow the pudding(s) to cool and remove foil covering and greaseproof covering. Re-cover with fresh greaseproof paper and clean calico squares secured with string and tied on top. On Christmas Day steam or boil for a further 3 hours (2 for a 1 pint pudding). Serve with brandy butter.

There is a lot of standing time in this recipe. It is worth keeping to this so that the liquids soak in properly and the flavours are brought out fully. I use unbleached calico for pudding cloths. This is stocked by John Lewis (amongst other places), and is quite cheap to buy. If you don't want to use pudding cloths then you can use kitchen foil for the second steaming too. These puddings keep extremely well. They can be used the following year. Left -overs can be frozen.

Fruity Oaty Crunch by Penny Baxter.

5oz Rolled Oats (or plain Porridge Oats)
5oz Self Raising Flour
5oz Caster Sugar
5oz Margarine
2oz dried fruit
1 tablespoon Milk
1 tablespoon Syrup (you could try honey as an alternative)

(One for those of you with dehydrators!!) Grease baking trays and
set oven to 180. Pour the flour into a bowl. Add the sugar and oats
and stir with a wooden spoon until it is all mixed well, then add in
and stir the dried fruit.
In a separate bowl add the melted margarine to milk and syrup to
make up the wet mix. Then gradually stir into the dry mix. You may
not need all of the wet mix. Once mixed as a fairly dry-ish mix,
which isn't too sticky, but does bind- form into small balls. Put these
onto the baking trays and flatten a little. Bake for around 20 minutes,
until the oaty crunchies look golden brown. Allow to cool for a few
minutes and then place onto a cooling rack.

E
Eggs

Pickled Eggs by Jacqui Bones.

8-10 hard boiled eggs
4 dried red chillies
Approx 3/4 pint pickling vinegar

Peel the eggs place in a jar so they fit neatly and do not extend over the top. Add 1-2 chillies to each jar cover with cold vinegar seal store for 3-4 weeks before use. Use within 3 months

Elderberries

Elderberry and Apple Jam by Jayne Hickling.

3 1/2 lb Elderberries (destalked weight and lightly rinsed)
3 1/2 lb Apples, (peeled and cored weight)
7lb Sugar.

Destalk and lightly rinse the Elderberries. Peel, core and chop up the apples and add to the Elderberries in a heavy based pan. Mash the fruit, until you can see the juices of the berries and turn on a low heat. Start to add the sugar a little at a time and stir into the fruit. Boil until the apples are soft and then "blitz" with a handheld blender. Leave to a rolling boil for around 10 minutes and remove any scum off the surface. Test the setting point and then pour into sterilised jars and seal.

F
Figs

<u>Roast Green Figs with Honey and Ricotta. By Vanessa Brett Davey.</u>

You can use other figs. Roasting the figs with honey really brings out the sweet taste.

6 figs
6 tbsp honey (thick or runny)
150g ricotta
50g thick Greek yoghurt
2 tbsp icing sugar
½ tsp vanilla extract or the seeds scraped from half a vanilla pod

Heat the oven to 200C. Cut an X into the top of each fig and squeeze gently to open it up. Trickle a little honey into each fig – reserve about half of it for serving – place in a tin and roast for 10-15 minutes, until hot and bubbling. Beat the ricotta with the yoghurt, icing sugar and vanilla until smooth. Spoon some of the mixture into the top of each fig and trickle on some more honey just before serving.

Image by Vanessa Brett Davey, Figs.

French Beans

Spring Rolls by Sharon Roberts Ramones.

Filo pastry sheets (spring roll wrappers)
Garlic about 4-5 cloves . Chop (finely)
Green beans. Chop (finely)
Carrott. Chop (finely)
Belly pork (optional you can use prawns or no meat at all)

Stir fry in big wok after 5 min make a well in the middle add 1 cup of water and a veg stock cube and salt, do not over cook they need to be al dentè leave to cool and drain then carefully take a sheet of filo pastry (spring roll wrappers) and put 1 spoon of veggies in a line then wrap. Once you have wrapped your veg you then put in fridge or freezer then when wanted shallow fry until golden brown (about 2-3min. Be warned the chopping is hard work but the end result is delicious.

Image by Sharon Roberts Ramones, Preparation for Spring Rolls.

G
Garlic

Wild Garlic Pesto by Vanessa Brett-Davey.

1 large handful wild garlic leaves, well washed and dried
2 tbsp. toasted pine kernels.
1 clove garlic, peeled and crushed
1 cup olive oil
4 tbsp. Parmesan Cheese (or vegetarian substitute hard cheese) freshly grated
Salt and fresh cracked pepper to taste
2 tbsp. lemon juice (to add at the last minute)

For best results us a pestle and mortar, but otherwise process the wild garlic, pine kernels, garlic and olive oil in a food processor. Add in the cheese to taste, add salt and pepper as required. Store the pesto in sterilised jar in the fridge. A squirt of lemon juice at the last minute brings a real kick to this pesto and anything served with it. Don't add lemon too early or the pesto will discolour.

Poor Man's Wild Garlic Pesto by Vanessa Brett-Davey.

2 Big Handfulls of Wild Garlic
50g Sunflower Seeds
3tbs Extra Virgin Olive Oil
Juice of 1 Lemon
Freshly Ground Black Pepper
Sea Salt to taste

Roughly chop the wild garlic, put in a food processor with all of the other ingredients and blend. Season to taste. Use as you would normal pesto and enjoy the extra garlic hit!!

Pickled Garlic by Helen Ruffles.

500g Garlic Cloves
1tsp Fennel Seed
About 12 Peppercorns (white, black, pink)
4-6 Bay Leaves
200ml Cider Vinegar
50g Granulated Sugar
Good pinch Saffron Strands

Have ready three warm, sterilised jars. Bring a large pan of water to the boil. Put in the whole garlic for a minute, which helps to loosen the outer skins. Remove from the water and pat dry. Break the garlic bulbs into individual cloves and pack them into the jars, alternating between the fennel seeds, peppercorns and bay leaves as you go. Put the vinegar, sugar and saffron into a pan. Bring to the boil and boil for a couple of minutes. Pour the hot vinegar over the garlic, then seal the jar with vinegar proof lids. Last a year in a cool dark cupboard.

Gherkin

<u>Saltgurkor by Anna Penelope.</u>

(Based on a Swedish recipes)
1 litre cold water
0.75 dl salt
1kg gherkins
10 blackcurrant leaves
Bunch of dill flowers

Dissolve the salt in the water and pour over the gherkins and leaves. Place the dill flowers upside down so that when the lid is closed they push down the gherkins into the water.

Gooseberries

<u>Gooseberry Curd by Moi MacMillan.</u>

680 g gooseberries topped & tailed
320 ml water
60 g butter
330 g granulated sugar
2 eggs.

Simmer the gooseberries gently in the water until soft. Sieve to remove seeds. Put the butter in a heatproof bowl & melt over a pan of simmering water. Add sugar and stir over heat until it's dissolved and then stand in bowl of cold water to cool. In a separate bowl, beat eggs lightly without frothing. When the butter and sugar mixture is cool, add it to the beaten eggs, stirring well .Strain through a sieve into a clean bowl. I combine all when cool and then sieve. Then return to heat by standing over bowl of hot water stirring constantly until begins thicken. When ready it should coat back of spoon, leaving a track if run your finger through it. Then put in jars as normal.

Green Beans

Green Bean Curry with Courgettes by Micheala Knight.

Handful of green Beans (any will do!!!)
2 Courgettes
1 red onion
2 cloves garlic
1tsp of each of following spices: Coriander, chilli powder, turmeric, salt, cumin.
8 Cardamom pods
3 Large fresh tomatoes (or one tin)
1 litre stock
400g Chickpeas
2 tbsp. Butter
Zest 1 Lemon

Chop and cook beans in water for about 6 mins, Drain, In another pan fry 8 bashed cardamom pods and a teaspoon of cinnamon, Then add chopped red onion, Chopped red pepper, 2 chopped garlic cloves and fry for about 5 mins. Add: A tablespoon of dried coriander, A teaspoon of hot chilli powder, A teaspoon of turmeric , A teaspoon of salt, A teaspoon of cumin. Coat onions. Then add 3 large chopped fresh tomatoes. A bit of water to stop sticking. After 5 mins add a litre of stock. The green beans and 400g of chickpeas. Bring to boil. Then lid on and cook on medium for 15 mins. Then lid off and cook for a further 15 mins so it thickens. Less if you like it more saucy. Ribbon courgette I used 2 using a peeler. Add salt, then fry on high for just a couple of mins. In micro melt a table spoon or 2 of butter. Then add zest of a lemon and juice of half a lemon to butter, pour over courgettes and add black pepper.

Green Bean Stew by Cara Kussan.

Onions
Peppers
Tomatoes
Tomato Puree
Green Beans
Salt and herbs
Potato
Water

Fry onions. Peppers and fresh tomatoes till soft add big dollop of tomato pure salt and mix herbs. Then add the green beans, I break them up loads. Toss in sauce. They will turn a different shade of green, fry them for five minutes. Then add one chopped peeled large potato. And enough water to cover and salt. Cook till soft. Serve with rice.

Image by Cara Kussan.

H
Honey

Mead by Finn Hannard.

2 Jars of Honey,
4 pints hand-warm water.
1 chopped up orange
Handful of sultanas
Heaped teaspoon of dried yeast (baking is fine, brewer's ideal).
Optional -- little bit of cinnamon, couple of cloves etc.

Don't worry if you don't have the correct equipment, as you can easily improvise!! Empty 2 jars of honey into a 4pt milk bottle, add hand-warm water to half way, shake to combine then top up to about 3" from the top. Add in half a chopped up orange, a handful of sultanas and a heaped teaspoon of dried yeast (baking is fine, brewer's ideal). Optional -- little bit of cinnamon, couple of cloves etc. Then if you haven't got the gnarly brewing airlocks, just put a balloon over the bottle opening, with a couple of pin pricks for the air to escape. Leave in a warmish place till it stops bubbling when you put your ear to it (the warmer, the faster this phase happens, I just had it at room temp and it took about 4 weeks). Then all you've got to do, is tip it into the bottles.

What I do is sterilise everything before use, and I use a funnel with a scrap of linen for a filter. Also before pouring, I cut the top off the milk bottle so I can get the bits out, and when I put the bottle down I lean it against something to keep it at the same angle, avoids disturbing the scum on the bottom.

Once it's bottled, it clears in about 2 or 3 weeks, you can drink it as soon as it's clear, but the longer you leave it the better. 3 months makes a good dessert tipple.

Horseradish

Horseradish Sauce by Jackie Hughes.

Horseradish sauce base (this will store for up to a year in a cool dry place)
225g (8oz) White Sugar
1 teaspoon salt
285ml (1/2 pint) distilled malt (white) vinegar
Grated horseradish root.

Dissolve the sugar and salt in the vinegar over a low heat and allow to cool. Take a sterilized Kilner type jar and put in a little of the minced horseradish, then pour on some syrup, repeating until the jar is full.

To make the actual sauce:

1 teaspoon mustard powder
Little Wine Vinegar
1 Tablespoon Horseradish sauce base
1 Tablespoon thick double cream or crème fraiche

Mix the mustard powder to a paste with a little wine vinegar. Mix the resultant mustard with the horseradish sauce base, then mix with the cream.

Horseradish Cream by Lynda Smith.

10 inch piece Horseradish
1x Tablespoon water
1 x Tablespoon whitewine vinegar
pinch of salt
Cream

Grate a 10 inch piece and mix with tablespoon of water, tablespoon white wine vinegar a large pinch of salt. Keep in fridge in tight blinded jar. Mix to taste with cream for fresh sauce. Keeps for a while. Be careful when grating it can be evil!

Horseradish Mayonnaise by Lou Duggan.

1 Root of Horseradish
Two cloves or Garlic
Mayonnaise

Grate one root of Horseradish and two cloves of garlic raw.
Add Mayonnaise.
Gorgeous with new potatoes or just a salad

K
Kale

Baked Pancake Cannelloni by Jayne Hickling.

Pancakes
4oz Plain Flour
Pinch Salt
1 Egg
Pancakes½ Pint milk
1x Large Handful of green leafy vegetables (Kale or Spinach)
125g Soft Cheese (Ricotta or Philadelphia)
Tomato Sauce
1x Medium Onion (Sliced)
1x Clove garlic (grated)
1x Courgette (halved and sliced)
Handful of Fresh Parsley (chopped)
½ tin Chopped tomatoes (200g) (Or three large tomatoes sliced and one tbsp Tomato Puree)
White Sauce
1 tsp butter
1 tsp cornflour
½ Pint milk
1 oz Cheddar Cheese (Grated)
A little oil for cooking and coating the baking dish.

Preheat the oven to 200c. Make the pancake batter (not including the leafy veg or soft cheese) and then make up five large pancakes and put to the side to cool down, in between pieces of greaseproof paper. Then make up the tomato sauce. Gentle cook down the onions, garlic, courgette and parsley in a little oil until soft but not browned and add the tinned tomatoes (or add the cut tomatoes and cook these down before adding the puree). Next make up the white sauce. Melt the butter in a pan and stir in the cornflour, add the milk and whisk on a high heat until the sauce thickens. Take one pancake at a time, spread over a dessert spoon of soft cheese per pancake. Next lay out the green leafy vegetables. Next top with a spoonful of the tomato sauce. Roll the pancake like a wrap, tucking in the ends as you roll and place the rolled savoury pancake into an ovenproof dish, which has been lightly brushed with oil. Repeat for all of the pancakes, laying them next to each other. Once all five filled savoury pancakes are in the baking dish, cover the pancakes with the white sauce. Finally add the grated cheddar cheese. Place in the preheated over for around 30minutes, or until the top has browned. This is brilliant if you make pancakes for any other reason and have any leftovers!!!

Image by Jayne Hickling. Baked Pancake with Kale Cannelloni

Kale Spread by Midge Holdsworth.

100g Kale,
1 boiled egg,
1/2 a shallot,
1/2 garlic clove,
1/2 tsp lemon juice,
2 tbsp extra-virgin olive oil.

Blanch the kale for 2-3 minutes until soft. Submerge in ice cold water to keep the bright green colour. Squeeze out the excess water and place the kale in a blender with all the other ingredients. Blitz and season. Keeps in the fridge for 3 days.

L
Leeks

<u>Leek, Mint and Feta Frittata by Stephen Baird.</u>

1 large onion, halved and sliced thinly
2 large leeks, sliced thinly
2 cloves of garlic (or a handful of wild garlic leaves) chopped
1/2 block of feta, crumbled
8 medium eggs whisked
Handful of mint

Fry the onions, leeks and garlic slowly in a large heavy frying pan. Whilst doing this whisk the eggs and add the feta and mint to this. When the leeks and onions are melty soft add the eggs and move around slightly, then cook for about 10 minutes on a low heat. Once it is semi-cooked through, put under a hot grill for another 5 minutes until browned.

<u>Leek and Carrot Tagliatelle by Jayne Hickling.</u>

250g Dried Tagliatelle
150g Carrots
4 Leeks
Oil

Cook the Tagliatelle until just cooked, but still "al dente". Strain and add a little olive oil of butter mixed into the drained pasta to stop it "glooping" together. Slice the Leeks and ribbon the carrots, by using a vegetable peeler.
In a large frying pan or wok, gently heat up the oil and add the sliced Leeks. Cook out, but avoid browning. Add to the pan the ribboned carrots and continue to soften on a gentle heat. Once the carrot ribbons and the leek is soft and "floppy", add the Tagliatelle. This can then be served as a base to grilled chicken, tuna or quorn pieces.

Lemon

Lemon Curd by Kelly Webster.

7oz Butter (unsalted)
1lb 9oz Granulated Sugar
5 Lemons- (Grated zest)
½ pint Lemon Juice (about 5 Lemons)
½ pint Beaten Eggs (about 4-5 eggs)

Place the butter, sugar, lemon zest and juice in a large bowl and microwave on full power for about 2 minutes or until the butter has melted and sugar has dissolved. (Or use the top of a double- boiler or a bowl over a pan of hot water) Add the beaten eggs and continue cooking in 1- minute bursts and stirring each time, keeping the temperature initially around 36C, reducing to 30 seconds for each burst. To thicken the mixture, once all of the egg has been slowly heated, raise the temperature to around 70c. To know if the mixture is thick enough, it should be able to coat the back of the spoon. Strain through a sieve into a wide- necked jug, to remove the lemon zest and any cooked egg bits. Put into cooled sterilised jars. Make sure that the jars are cool- otherwise it will over cook the egg and you may get eggy bits. Store in the fridge.

Image by Vanessa Brett Davey. Lemon Curd

Lemon Drizzle Cake (Gluten free) by Rachel Laing.

2 tbsp lemon juice
8oz gluten free self raising flour
2 tsp baking powder
8oz vegetable oil
8oz caster sugar
4 eggs
Lemon curd
Drizzle
4oz sifted icing sugar
6 tsp lemon juice

Put all cake ingredients (not Lemon curd) in a bowl and mix until smooth and creamy. Divide the mixture between your two pre-prepared cake tins. (if using round tins cake will be taller than mine) Place in your pre-heated oven (170 fan) for about 40 minutes. Once completely cool spread a large amount of lemon curd (either homemade or bought) onto the base & gently sandwich the top of the cake on top. Make your lemon glace icing for the top of your cake by combining your icing sugar with lemon juice. When icing is smooth and glossy (not too runny), pour or spoon it over the cake. (I often find its better with glace to start from the middle as it will run towards to edges) Grate some lemon zest on top of the icing. Allow the glace icing to set by leaving it in a cool place for only about 30 minutes (always keep it cool).

M
Marrow

<u>Marrow and Chilli Jam by Teresa Witham.</u>

1kg marrow
100g. chilli
100ml white vinegar (although using balsamic vinegar gives a nice twist!!)
100g onion
1kg sugar

Blitz the veg in a processor or finely dice, mix everything together in pan, bring to the boil and boil rapidly until thick and the moisture has reduced.
Beware as it thickens it can turn in to an erupting volcano as you stir.
When thick put into jars and put the lids on straight away!
Great with cheese
*alter chilli content to taste, make sure you know how hot your chilli's are to start with!

Image by Jayne Hickling. Marrow and Chilli Jam.

Marrow Loaf by Celia Stapleton.

275g cups sugar (your choice)
80g cup butter, softened
225g cups grated courgette/marrow
80ml cup water
2 eggs
195g cups flour
1 tsp baking soda
1 tsp salt
½ tsp cinnamon
½ tsp ground cloves
1 tsp vanilla
½ tsp baking powder
50g cup coarsely chopped walnuts or other favourite nut (or no nuts if you want)
75g cup raisins

Preheat oven to 180C, and grease the bottoms only of 2 loaf pans.
Mix sugar and butter, stir in courgette/ marrow, water and eggs.
Mix in flour, baking soda, salt, cinnamon, cloves, vanilla and baking powder. Lastly stir in nuts and raisins, and pour into baking pans.
Bake 45 minutes, till pick comes out clean from centre of loaf.
Cool for about 5 minutes before removing from pans.

Marrow and Ginger Jam by Merle Prewett.

3 lb (1.5 kg) marrow
1 lb (500 g) cooking apples
2 oz (50 g) root ginger
Juice of 2 lemons (or 4 tablespoons of bottled Lemon Juice)
3 lb (1.5 kg) jam sugar

Peel the marrow, discard the seeds and cut into cubes. Peel and core the apples and cut the flesh into cubes.
Place in pan and steam until tender and then mash. Add the lemon juice. Bruise the root ginger and wrap in a piece of muslin and place in the pan. Add the sugar, simmer and stir until dissolved. Bring to the boil and boil for about 30 minutes, stirring occasionally as the pulp thickens and setting point is reached. Pot into hot sterilized jars immediately and cover.
Makes about 4 lbs (2 kg) of jam.

Stuffed Marrow by Sue Popkin.

Marrow
Onion
Garlic
Minced Meat/ Quorn
Tomato Puree
Tin Chopped Tomatoes
Chilli or Paprika
Basil
Cheese (optional for grating and topping off)

Chop small onion with garlic and cook in a small amount of oil for 5 minutes until soft. Add meat (or Quorn) and mix together and cook meat or Quorn through for 5 Minutes. Add 2 tbsp of tomato puree and tin chopped tomatoes, add salt, pepper. You can also add either chilli or paprika if you want it a bit spicy. Then add basil. Mix together and taste and add more seasoning if needed, or maybe some mixed herbs for your preferred taste. Cook down so most of the juice has reduced. Take out the seeds from the marrow, peel the skin off and cut in to two halves. Next add the mince/ Quorn mix. Bake in oven at 180 for about 40 minutes until marrow is cooked through and meat is brown. If you have some sauce left over reheat and pour over when serving.

Image by Davina Lynn. Stuffed Marrow.

Marrow Pickle by Linda Ford.

2 kg marrow
salt
1½ tablespoons ground ginger
1½ tablespoons dry mustard
1½ tablespoons turmeric
4 onions, finely chopped
6 whole cloves
1litre 250ml malt vinegar
Remove the seeds and cut the unpeeled marrow into squares.
Sprinkle with salt and let stand overnight, then drain well.

Combine the remaining ingredients in a saucepan and boil for 10
minutes, add the marrow and boil slowly until the marrow is tender.
It can be thickened with a little flour mixed with vinegar but this is
not really necessary. Spoon into hot, clean jars and seal.

Surprise Lemon and Ginger Jam by Linda Ford.

Weigh the marrow/courgette first and adjust the recipe proportionately: 1 lemon and 30g unpeeled ginger to 40-45g vegetable. The weight of sugar should be the same as unpeeled marrow/courgette. The amounts of the ingredients below depend and changed depending on the amount of vegetables you use!!

Marrow or courgette (peeled, deseeded and in small dice)
White sugar
Lemons
Fresh root ginger (peeled and grated)

Peel the marrow, remove the seeds and cut into small dice. Place in a large saucepan. Remove the lemon zest, (being careful not to remove any white pith) and set aside. Cut the lemon in half and squeeze into a jug. Place the empty lemon shells and pips into a small muslin bag (or foot section of a clean pair of tights). Add a small amount of the lemon juice to the pan, cover with a lid and gently cook the marrow until transparent. If necessary add some more lemon juice to stop the marrow sticking. Spoon the marrow and any collected liquids into a blender and liquidise until smooth. Alternatively the mixture can be mashed for a slightly coarser texture or, providing the dice are very small, left as it is. Peel the ginger, grate using the large holes of the grater and add to the lemon zest. Add the ginger peelings and any very fibrous pieces to the small bag with the leftover lemon pieces. Return the marrow mixture to the same pan, add the remaining lemon juice, the lemon and ginger. Stir in and dissolve the sugar. Knot the bag of bits and add it to the pan. Bring the mixture to the boil and then turn down to a rolling simmer. Stir regularly, pressing down on the bag of bits occasionally and reduce until the mixture has reached setting point. Test for a set by putting a half teaspoon of jam on a saucer from the freezer. If, once it has cooled a little, it wrinkles when pushed with a finger, it should be ready to pot. If not ready then leave for 5 minutes and try again. This usually takes me around 25 minutes.

Marrow Burgers/ Sausages by Jayne Hickling.

This recipe is very adaptable as a basic vegetarian staple. This is because you can shape it into burgers/ patties, sausages or even "meat"balls. This means that once cooked, they can be used in a variety of dishes.

1lb Marrow (peeled and seeded)
125g Onion- diced
500g Carrots
Porridge Oats and Flour
4 tbsp. Soya sauce
Vegetable oil for cooking
3 tsp Cumin

Grate the marrow into a bowl and add the diced onion and then mix together. Add in the oats, a little bit at a time, stirring into the marrow and onion mixture. You need enough oats to bring the mixture together, but not too much that it becomes dry. Add in the soya sauce, until a nice dark brown colour has been achieved. You may need to add some more oats, as the consistency needs to be dough-like. Form into patties, sausages or balls and fry in the vegetable oil to hold the shape- if they are to be frozen, take them out of the pan at this point and dry on a kitchen towel before placing in freezer bags. If they are to be used straight away, cook on until crispy on the outside. To cook from frozen, you will need to defrost and then shallow fry, as they don't reheat well in the oven.

Mixed Seeds

Granola by Jayne Hickling.

750 ml wholemeal oats
30 grams Flaked Almonds
30 grams sunflower seeds
30 grams Pumpkin Seeds
½ teaspoon ground cinnamon

½ teaspoon ground ginger (optional)
¼ teaspoon salt
80 grams sultanas (or your choice of dried fruits)
125 ml Honey (or maple syrup is nice!!)
125ml Extra Virgin Olive Oil (It must be extra virgin, as this has a lower cooking point then other oils)

Preheat oven to 150C. Mix all of the dry ingredients together in a large bowl, including any of the spices. In another bowl mix together the wet ingredients and then add this to the dry mix. Spread out mixture on baking sheet and bake for about 30-35 minutes. You want it to be turning brown, just watch the edges as they may "catch" first. Take the trays out of the oven and allow them to cool before crumbling into whatever size chunks you like. Let cool then store in an air tight container.

Mixed Vegetables

Spiced Tomato, Courgette and Red Pepper Chutney by Alex Vogler- El Masri.

1 tsp cumin seeds (or ground cumin)
2 tsp coriander seeds (or ground coriander)
4 tbsp olive oil
5 medium sized Courgettes
2 large onions, diced finely
4 red peppers, cut into approx 1 cm dice (I like my chutney chunky but if you like yours finer feel free to use a food processor to do the chopping)
1.4kg ripe tomatoes, cut into approx 1 cm dice
8 cloves garlic, crushed
4 tbsp ginger (a chunk of ginger the size of about 4 wine corks), grated
8 tbsp soft brown sugar or demerara sugar
8 tbsp red wine vinegar or cider vinegar
Grated zest and juice of 4 oranges
1 tsp dried crushed red chilli flakes (optional if you like your chutney with a kick)

Lightly crush the cumin and coriander seeds (if using) in a pestle and mortar and toast them in a dry frying pan until they start to release their aroma, then remove them from the heat and set aside. If you're using ground spices, these will also need to be lightly toasted. Pour the oil into a large pan and add the diced onions and toasted spices. Cook for a few minutes until they are slightly translucent. Now add all of the remaining ingredients and bring to the boil. Turn down to a simmer until it thickens. Keep stirring it frequently so that it doesn't stick to the pan. Test to see if your chutney is thick enough by dragging your spoon down the centre of the pan, if the chutney stays "split", you're done. This might take around 30-45 minutes, but it depends on the amount of "water" and fluids inside the vegetables and may take longer. Once it is thick enough from the spoon test, put into sterilised jars.

Veg Saag by Nan Roberts Massey.

New potatoes cut in half or square if bigger,
2 Cloves Garlic
Curry Powder
Tin Chopped Tomatoes
Spinach

New potatoes cut in half or square if bigger, large onion. Par boil potatoes fry onion and two cloves garlic add curry powder and tin of chopped tomatoes, add potatoes and a squeeze of tomato paste or tomato sauce add spinach and simmer till cooked salt and pepper.

Mixed Vegetable Pickle by Jacqui Bones.

1 small cauliflower
2-3 courgettes
½ cucumber
2 onions peeled and sliced or ½ lb pickling onions
4-6 oz French beans trimmed and blanched
Salt
1 pint pickling vinegar
Optional for extra flavour
1 small green or red pepper
1 level tsp whole spice

Cut the cauliflower in to small florets, dice the courgettes cucumber cut the beans into ½ inch lengths deseed the pepper. The total weight should be about 2lb.
Place all the vegetables into a large bowl sprinkler liberally with salt cover and leave for 24-36 hours wash all the salt off and drain very well. Pack the vegetables neatly into clean jars, but not too tightly, with a few all spice. Then fill the jars with cold vinegar store for two weeks.

Piccalilli by Jacqui Bones.

2lb prepared vegetables (cucumber courgettes pickling onions cauliflower marrow beans green tomatoes etc)
5oz salt
3oz caster sugar
½ oz dry mustard
1 level teaspoon ground ginger
1 pint pickling vinegar
1oz cornflower
1 level tablespoon turmeric

Dice the cucumber courgettes peel onions cut cauliflower into small florets deseed marrow and dice slice beans cut tomatoes into small pieces. Layer the vegetables with salt in a large bowl cover and leave for 24 hours drain off salt solution and wash vegetables, drain well. Mix sugar mustard and ginger with ¾ pint of vinegar in a large pan bring to the boil add the vegetables bring back to the boil cover and simmer for 10-15 minutes the vegetables should be tender and crisp blend cornflower turmeric and remaining vinegar add to pan bring back to the boil for about 2 minutes. Pack vegetables into sterilised jars and fill up with sauce seal immediately store for at 2 weeks.
Makes 2 ½ -3lbs

Image by Hazel Turner, Piccalilli.

Warming Cheesy Soup by Helen Ruffles.

1 large onion, finely chopped
3 large diced potatoes, rinsed
4 large grated carrots
Stock, approx 1.5L
4 leeks, halved lengthwise and finely sliced
6 tbsp quick cook oats
230 g hard cheese, (I use cheddar).
Seasoning
Chives/parmesan rind optional

Bring stock to boil. (With or without parmesan rind). Add potatoes and onions and simmer about 8 minutes. Add leeks and carrots and simmer approx 8 minutes. Add oats, simmer 5 minutes. Remove rind and blitz. Add cheese. Season and add chives if using.
(If this is being made for vegetarians- then look out for the rennet content, especially in parmesan, as this is typically not vegetarian)

Freezes well.

Winter Vegetable Soup with Croutons by Jayne Hickling.

1 Onion
1 Carrot
1 medium potato
2 Cubes of Frozen Curly
Kale
1 Stock cube
1 Handful of parsley
1 tsp ground Coriander
1 tsp paprika
salt to taste
white and black pepper
to taste
oil
1 tsp flour

Image by Jayne Hickling, Winter Vegetable Soup with Croutons

Cut fresh vegetables in to small cubes and then sweat off the fresh vegetables in a small amount of oil, with the chopped parsley. Add in the vegetable stock and the frozen cubes of curly kale. (look at instructions for blanching leafy veg). Cover the pan and leave to simmer, until all of the vegetables are soft. Add in the seasoning to taste. Finally, in a separate bowl, mix the flour with a tsp of water to make a paste. Add this to the soup as a thickener.

Croutons.

Take one slice of bread (I used the "knobby"!) and cut into small cubes. Put a small amount of oil into a frying pan and bring up the heat. Add the small cubed pieces of bread and lightly "fry", tossing the cubes to make sure they don't burn. Add to your bowl of soup when ready to serve.

Curly Kale, Cabbage and Potato Soup by Sue Chambers.

1 med/large onion or mixture of onion and leeks,
4 med/large curly kale leaves,
1/2 small cabbage,
3 sticks celery,
3 to 4 small potatoes,
salt,
pepper,
paprika,
1 vegetable stock cube or 2 depending on amount you make,
3 or 4 small garlic cloves and parsley.

Cut and sauté the whole lot in butter and olive oil. Cover mixture to around 1 inch above vegetables and high simmer until cooked then blend. If too thick add a bit of water. Add a bit of parsley/coarse ground black pepper on top to garnish.

Indian Spiced Marrow, Beetroot and Tomato Chutney by Teresa Witham.

2lb Sugar
2lb Marrow (Deseeded and peeled)
8oz Tomatoes
8oz Raisins
8oz Beetroot (peeled)
1 chilli
1tsp coriander seed
1tsp Mustard Seeds
1tsp cumin seeds
5 ground cardamom pods husks removed
1tsp Nigella seeds
1tsp Celery Seeds
1tsp Salt
1tsp Garam Masala
1¼ pint Malt Vinegar

Blitz all vegetables in a processor or finely chop. Grind all spices in a pestle and mortar. Put everything in a heavy based pan bring slowly to the boil and boil rapidly until reduced thick and stays divided when a spoon is drawn through it. Put into warm sterilized jars and seal immediately, lovely straight away amazing if left to mature for at least 6 weeks.

Potato, Red Onion and Cheddar Pasties by Sarah Williams.

1 large potato, cut into 1cm dice
2 carrots, cut into 1cm dice
300g jar caramelised onion chutney
1 tbsp thyme leaf, chopped
1 tbsp Dijon mustard
140g mature cheddar, grated
500g block shortcrust pastry
Beaten egg, for brushing
Poppy seeds, for sprinkling

Heat oven to 190C/170C fan/gas 5. Line a baking tray with baking parchment. Boil the potato and carrots in salted water for 5 mins until tender. Drain well and tip into a mixing bowl. Add the chutney, thyme, mustard, cheese and some seasoning, and gently mix to combine. Put in the fridge to cool. Roll out the pastry to the thickness of a £1 coin, then cut out 8 x 13cm squares. Divide the filling between the squares and brush the pastry edges with the egg. Bring together the 4 corners of each square in the middle, then press all the seams together like a square envelope. Brush with more egg and sprinkle over the poppy seeds. Put the pasties on the baking tray and bake for 30 mins until golden.

Roasted Vegetable Pasta by Helen Godfrey.

olive oil
2 red Onions, cut into wedges
2 medium Peppers, deseeded and cut into chunks
2 medium Courgette, thickly sliced
1 individual Chilli, Green or Red, (preferably red), deseeded and finely chopped
2 sprig(s) Thyme, Fresh
4 garlic bulbs (peeled and crushed)
390 g Artichoke hearts, cooked, in brine, drained
12 Cherry Tomatoes, on the vine
150 g White pasta, dry, shapes
1 pinch Salt, and freshly ground black pepper

Preheat the oven to 180C. Put the olive oil into a large roasting pan and add the onion, peppers, courgette, garlic and chilli. Toss to coat in the oil. Season and add the herb sprigs. Roast in the oven for 30 minutes. Once everything else is cooked, stir in the artichokes and put the cherry tomatoes on top. Put the dish back into the oven and carry on roasting the vegetables whilst the pasta cooks. Drain the pasta and stir add to the vegetables and stir through.

Bread and Butter Pickle by Linda Phillips.

1 ½ lb Pickling Cucumbers
1 ¼ lb Onions, Sliced 5mm (¼ in thick)
12 oz red or yellow peppers, sliced 5mm (1/4 in) thick
3 tbsp Salt
1 Litre (1 ¾ pints) cider vinegar, white wine vinegar, or malt vinegar
1 lb light soft brown or white sugar
2 tsp ground turmeric
1 tbsp mustard seeds
2 tsp dill seeds

Put the cucumbers in a bowl and pour boiling water over them. Drain, refresh under cold running water and drain again. Slice the cucumbers into 1cm (½ in) thick pieces Put the cucumbers, sliced onions and peppers in a large glass bowl and sprinkle with the salt. Mix well, then cover the bowl with a clean cloth and leave to stand overnight. The next day, drain off the liquid in the bowl. Rinse the vegetables under cold running water and drain well. Taste a piece of cucumber, if it is too salty, cover the vegetables with more cold water and leave to stand for about 10 minutes then drain, rinse and drain again. Put the vinegar, sugar, ground turmeric, mustard seeds and dill seeds in the preserving pan. Bring to the boil, and boil rapidly for 10 minutes. Add the drained vegetables, return to the boil then remove from the heat. Pack the pickle into the hot sterilised jars, then seal. The pickle is ready to eat immediately.

Image by Jayne Hickling, Gardener's Pizza.

Image by Jayne Hickling, Vegetable Korma.

Vegetable Samosas by Jayne Hickling.

2 Green Chillies
2 Cloves garlic
2 ½ cm ginger root
½ tsp ground turmeric
¼ tsp ground coriander
½ tsp ground cumin
1 tbsp oil
1 onion, sliced
4oz Peas
4oz carrots, chopped
4oz potatoes, chopped
½ tsp salt
15ml tbsp water
12 oz plain flour
pinch of salt
4 tbsp water
oil for deep frying

Grind the spices to a paste. Heat the oil and fry the onions until browned. Add the peas, carrots and potatoes and fry for 2 minutes. Add the ground spices, salt and water. Cover and simmer until the vegetables are tender and the water is absorbed. Mix the flour and salt and add enough water to make a soft dough. Divide the dough into small balls, then roll them into 8cm circles. Cut in half and shape into cones, sealing the edges together with a little water. Spoon the vegetable mixture into the cones and seal the edges carefully. Deep fry in the hot oil until brown. Makes loads, but they oddly taste better once they've been frozen and then defrosted in the oven!

Gardener's Pizza by Jayne Hickling.

Pizza Base-
8oz flour
2 teaspoons (1 pouch) yeast
1 teaspoon salt
1 teaspoon sugar
2 teaspoons olive oil
8 fl oz warm water
Topping-
Tomato Puree (could be homemade!)
1 clove garlic
handfull of spinach
2 small florets broccoli
3 asparagus spear sliced in half
2 teaspoons peas
1/2 small Onion
Cheese
Garlic infused olive oil to dribble on top!!!

Mix the flour, salt and sugar together. Add the dried yeast and mix again.
Add the olive oil and crumble together. Next add the warm water- you may
not need all of the water, so just add until a smooth dough has been made,
which isn't sticky. Cover with cling film and leave for half an hour in a
warm place.
Once risen, punch the dough back and then roll out onto a floured surface.
Spread the tomato puree over the base. Put the spinach on top of the tomato
puree and then sprinkle the cut and sliced vegetables, finishing with the
spears of asparagus and top with cheese and the garlic infused oil if using.
Put into a preheated oven 180-200 degrees for approx 15 minutes.
Can be made with a pizza stone, pre-heat the stone in the oven. Prepare the
pizza on a surface sprinkled with polenta, so that it can be easily moved to
the pizza stone in the oven.
Any spare dough left over, can also be used to make dough balls, which are
really lovely dipped in garlic butter or garlic mayonnaise!!

Vegetable Korma by Jayne Hickling.

Paste
1 Onion
2 tablespoons vegetable oil
1 tsp cumin
1 tsp coriander
1 tsp ginger
1 tsp garam masala
1 tsp dried chillies
1 tsp curry powder
1 tsp turmeric
1 clove garlic
Sauce
1 tin tomatoes
2 tablespoons desiccated coconut
1 tablespoon vegetable oil
Carrots
Courgette
Cauliflower
Broccoli.

I love this. It does have quite a lot of spices in, but once they're in the store-cupboard, they're there for a while and make a fair few batches of this. Not strictly a korma- but that's what I call it- as it does pack a bit of heat, but very flavourful! Put the oil into a pan and bring to sizzling point. Add the onions with all of the spices, which can be fresh and ground in a pestle and mortar. Once the onion has turned "clear" and the spices are cooked, add the desiccated coconut and the tin tomatoes. Remove from the heat and place in a separate container to "blitz" with a processor. I know I've put tinned tomatoes in the recipe- but they do really need to be tinned, unless you have a homemade plain tomato sauce, without the skins already prepared.

Put the peeled and sliced vegetables into the pan that you made the sauce in and heat gently with a little vegetable oil. After around two minutes, add the sauce, cover the pan and leave to simmer until the vegetables are softened. Add a little milk (optional) then continue to heat for a further couple of minutes before serving with either rice or nann bread.

Mushrooms

<u>Garlic Mushroom Soup by Nan Roberts Massey.</u>

250gm mushrooms
1 large sweet potato
1 vegetable cube
1 ½ pint water
2 garlic cloves.

Chop up the mushrooms and sweet potato and sweet off in a little oil in a pan. Pour in the water with the stock cube. Whilst this is simmering. Melt butter with two cloves garlic and chopped parsley. Tear off little chunks of bread soak in garlic butter then put on a hot tray in hot oven to crisp. When mushrooms and sweet potato are soft, blend it. Add swirl of cream or milk. Serve with garlic croutons on top.

<u>Roasted Garlic Mushrooms by Alec Popkin.</u>

16 even-sized open cup mushrooms, stalks cut level
3 tbsp corn or vegetable oil
1/4 c unsalted butter, softened
3 cloves garlic, chopped very finely
2 tbsp fresh thyme, chopped
1 1/2 tbsp lemon juice
salt and freshly ground black pepper to taste
1/4 c fresh breadcrumbs.

Preheat the oven to 200C. Lightly fry the mushrooms, cap-side down, in hot oil for 20 seconds. Arrange the mushrooms in a shallow roasting tin with the stalks facing upwards. Mix together the butter, garlic, thyme, lemon juice and seasoning. Spoon a little garlic butter on to each mushroom, then lightly press the breadcrumbs on top. You can either refrigerate for later use, or cook immediately in the oven for 10 minutes.

N

Nasturtium Seeds

Poor Man's Capers by Rebecca Willmott.

Nasturtium Seeds
50g salt
450g water
Spiced Vinegar

Place the seed pods in a brine solution of 50g salt to 450g water for 24 hours. Then rinse and pack into warm sterile jars, pour over boiling spiced vinegar and seal.

O
Onions

<u>Pickled Onions by Jacqui Bones.</u>

4lb pickling onions
4oz salt
1 1/2 pints cold water
Approx 1 quart of pickling vinegar
4 oz caster sugar

Peel the onions place in a bowl combine the salt and water and pour over to cover the onions leave for 24 hours. Pour off the solution rinse the onions thoroughly and shake dry. Pack into clean jars and cover with cold vinegar. Can be eaten after 2 weeks, but best within 6 months. For sweet pickled onions dissolve the sugar in ¼ pint vinegar leave to cool and add to remainder vinegar and continue as above. Makes 4 lb.

Image by Linda Phillips.

Christmas Chutney by Jayne Hickling.

2lbs (900g) onions, sliced
2lb Cooking apples, peeled and chopped
1 pkt fresh cranberries 12oz
2 pints cider vinegar (although malt will do)
Zest 2 oranges
1oz fresh ginger chopped finely
1tbsp coarse sea salt
½ tsp mixed spice   Dried ingredients
2lb naturally dried apricots coarsely chopped
1 pkt of dates pitted and chopped 6oz
1lb raisins
Juice of 8 oranges or 1pint orange juice.
You will also need:
2lb Granulated sugar

First, put the dried fruit into a bowl and pour the orange juice over it, to soak. Place the first block of ingredients (the fresh ingredients) into a saucepan and cook gently, until the onion is pale and see-through and the cranberries have given up some of their colour, turning the contents pale pink. Add the dried fruit - which will have absorbed much of the orange juice - to the saucepan, together with the sugar. Bring up to a simmering boil, stirring frequently so the contents don't 'catch' on the bottom of the saucepan.
As the liquid appears to thicken, reduce the heat slightly, then put the chutney into sterilised jars and seal.

Pickled Onions with Balsamic Vinegar and Honey by Jayne Hickling.

2lb shallots or small pickling onions
2oz salt
3tsp allspice
1 tsp whole cloves
1 large cinnamon stick
12 black peppercorns
1 small piece root ginger, peeled & sliced
1 ½ pints malt vinegar
2 tbsp clear honey
½ pint balsamic vinegar

Peel the onions/shallots and place them in a large glass or ceramic bowl with the salt. Stir well to coat the onions, then cover and leave for 24 hours. Tie the spices in a muslin bag, put into a saucepan with the vinegar, balsamic and honey and bring to the boil. Remove from heat, and leave to cool overnight. Remove the spices. Rinse the onions well and pat dry with absorbent kitchen paper. Pack into sterilised jars and add enough spiced pickling vinegar to cover completely. Seal and store for at least two weeks before using. I also like these with cucumber, which will also need to be steeped in salt before treating, as they are so full of natural water.

Fresh Onion Chutney by Heidi Whyley.

500g (1lb) large, sweet purple or white onions, sliced very thinly,
1 tbsp of salt,
1-2 fresh green or red chillies, deseeded and finely chopped,
3tbsp white vinegar or cider vinegar
2 tbsp chopped mint or coriander,
1 tsp of novella seeds.

Put onions in a colander and sprinkle the salt. Mix well and leave to drain for an hour. Squeeze the onion to extract as much moisture as possible, mix with rest of the ingredients and leave to stand for an hour allowing the flavour to develop. The Chutney is ready to go.

Image by Jayne Hickling, Onion Bhaji and Cucumber and Onion Raita.

115

Onion Bhaji by Jayne Hickling.

Onion Mix
2 tbsp olive oil
4 Medium Onions (sliced 2mm thick)
½ tsp turmeric powder
½ tsp ground coriander
¼ tsp ground ginger
¼ tsp ground cumin
¼ tsp hot chilli powder (can be more depending on heat tolerance)
For the Batter
2 tbsp garam masala
10 tbsp gram flour (I use plain flour which works fine if you can't get gram flour)
½ teaspoon salt
¼ tsp ground cumin
½ tsp ground coriander
½ tsp garlic powder (I used one glove of fresh garlic)
½ tsp turmeric powder
Water as needed (I use around ¼ pint of water- but it depends on the variables of your ingredients)

Preheat deep fryer or cooking oil to 180c.

For the onion mixture, warm the oil in a frying pan over a medium heat. Add the onions and cook and stir until just soft (do not brown). This allows them to be formed into balls more easily. Add all of the spices and coat in the frying pan.

For the batter, Mix the ingredients together in a large bowl, gradually adding the water last to achieve the consistency of thin peanut butter. Mix in the onions so that they are evenly coated in batter. I add my onions straight from the frying pan, with the juices. Using two dessert spoons, form into balls and carefully place into the hot oil. Mine look more like a slightly runny batter and went into the oil like drop scones rather than fully formed balls. Cook until a deep golden colour. Make sure some of the outside looks crispy, as you want to be sure that the flour has cooked inside the bhajis or you get a "floury" taste. Remove from the oil and allow to drain on kitchen paper before serving. Can be frozen and reheated in the oven.

Onion Marmalade by Heidi Whyley.

1.25 kg (2 and 1/2 lbs onions, sliced in to rings
3 tbsp of salt
1kg (2lbs) preserving or granulated sugar
500 ml (17 oz) vinegar
1 1/2 tsp cloves tied in a piece of muslin
2 tsp caraway seeds

Sprinkle the onions with the salt and leave to stand for an hour.
Rinse and dry. Put the sugar, vinegar and the muslin bag in the pan.
Bring to the boil and simmer for 5 minutes. Add the onions and
caraway seeds. Return to boil and skim, reduce the heat to minimum
and cook for 2 ½ hours, or until the syrup is thick and the onions are
translucent and golden brown.

Remove the pan from the heat and leave for a few minutes. Ladle the
mixture into the hot, sterilized jars, then seal. The marmalade is
ready to eat immediately but improves with keeping.

Orange

Spiced Orange Rings by Jacqui Bones.

8 firm oranges
¾ pickling vinegar
1lb white sugar
¾ tsp whole cloves

Wipe the oranges do not peel cut into thin slices about ¼ inch thick. Put into pan in layers and barely cover with water bring to the boil and simmer for 25 minutes or until the rind is tender. Drain well and put the cooking liquor back into the pan with the vinegar sugar and cloves heat gently until the sugar has dissolved then bring to the boil for five minutes. Add the orange rings a few at a time and simmer until the rind becomes clear remove the rings straight to warmed jars arranging repeat with the rest of the rings. Boil the syrup until it begins to thicken leave to cool a little while. Pour into the jars to cover the oranges adding a few cloves (optional). Seal and store for 2 weeks.

Seville Orange Marmalade by Jane Scrivens.

1kg Seville Oranges
2 Lemons
1.5kg granulated sugar
2 litres water

Wash the fruit, halve and squeeze out juice and pips into a separate bowl. Tie the pips in a muslin. Slice the fruit thinly and place in a large bowl with the water, extracted juice and bag of pips. Cover and leave to stand overnight. This is really important, as otherwise the skins will remain tough and will not be edible in the final marmalade. Next day, pour the contents of the bowl into a large preserving pan and bring to the boil. Turn the heat down and simmer slowly until the peel is soft and the liquid has reduced by about half. Remove the bag of pips, squeeze out the liquid into the pan. Add the sugar to the pan. Stir continuously until the sugar dissolves. Boil rapidly for 15 minutes until setting point is reached. Test for setting using a clean, cold saucer. Pot and seal in the usual way.

P
Parsnips

<u>Parsnip and Apple Soup by Cid Eric.</u>

1lb apples peeled and quartered
1lb parsnips peeled and chopped
2 medium onions
2 cloves garlic
1ltr vegetable stock
Milk to thin the finished soup

Soften the onions and garlic in a little oil, add apples, parsnips and stock cook until parsnips are soft (I put mine in the slow cooker on high for a couple of hours whilst I did something else). Blitz with a stick blender or food processor, thin to your liking with the milk add salt and pepper to taste.
Serve with parsnip crisps a drizzle of olive oils and some good bread. Awesome!

Pears

Pear and Ginger Chutney by Anne Roseveare.

1.5kg firm pears (peeled, cored, chopped 1/2inch pieces)
500ml cider vinegar
450g brown sugar (demerara)
200g onions (chopped small)
225g raisins
125g fresh ginger root (peeled, chopped 1/4inch pieces)
2tsp ground cinnamon
1tsp whole cloves (packed solid)
1tsp cayenne or chilli powder.

Put the vinegar in the pan and add the pear (stops it browning before you have a chance to get them all chopped), onion and raisins. Get it heating up before you add the sugar (easier to dissolve it), mix in the ginger and spices, and bring it to a boil. Simmer until it thickens (stir to make sure it doesn't stick and burn) then put into sterile jars.

Pear Chutney by Devina Lynn.

Used about 12 pears,
Chucked in a few apples,
100 grams brown sugar
Cinnamon,
200 grams chopped dates ,
Malt vinegar just covering fruit

Peel and core the apples and pears. Chop up all of the fruit, including the dates and add the vinegar, so that it is just covering the fruit. Mix in the sugar and cinnamon. Cook until the fruit is soft and then simmer until the liquid is reduced and the chutney has thickened. Put into sterilised jars.

Peas

Pea and Ham Soup by Jane Scrivens.

300g split peas
250g Serrano ham (or 100g bacon and 150g pork)
2 onions
1 litre of ham stock
½ litre water
2 large carrots
3 sticks celery
1 large potato

Sauté one onion in a little butter until soft with the stockpot lid on. (I use the fat from the top of the home made ham stock). Add the stock, water, peas and the ham chopped into small cubes. Bring to the boil then simmer gently for one hour, stirring occasionally. Add the carrots, celery, potato and second onion, all finely chopped. (I used some left over potato from the previous day). Add leeks instead of onion at this stage if you have any to hand. Simmer for 30 minutes or so, stirring frequently. This recipe is loosely based on Dutch 'Snert'. Other recipes specify 150g pork and 100g bacon instead of Serrano ham but I was using up a large ham! If you don't have ham stock then use 1½ litres water and some stock cubes. This soup is fairly salty, so you probably won't need to add any extra salt.

Plums

Spiced Plum Jelly by Nikki Mason.

1.6kg red plums
400ml cider vinegar
150ml port
1 cinnamon
8 cloves
8 cardamom pods
Granulated sugar (amount depends on variations!!)

Cut up plums and put in a preserving pan with the stones. Add port,
vinegar and spices. Boil for 1hr on a low heat. Strain through a sieve,
(if you like a clearer jelly use muslin) should be about 800ml juice
add 500g sugar to every 600ml juice. Boil until setting point reached.
Test on a saucer, depends on plums ripeness, took a little longer to
reach setting point. Have in past had to re-boil to get plums to set
have also added lemon juice. Once you have made first time you will
know for next time. Pour into sterilised jars and seal amazing with
roasts especially turkey and chicken.

Old Mrs Evans' Chutney by Nan Roberts Massey.

1 ½ lbs plums
1 ½ lbs Bramley apples,
8 oz red or green tomatoes,
1 lb raisins,
8 oz onions

Blitz all or chop as fine as u can. I leave half the raisins whole. One
and half lbs dark brown sugar, 4oz preserved ginger, 2 garlic cloves,
5gm of chilli flakes optional. 1 ½ tablespoon of salt and one pint
malt vinegar. Keep stirring then simmer stirring occasionally for one
and half hours. It'll look like chutney. Then into hot jars.

Plum and Blackberry Jam by Kayleigh Shaw.

1lb plums
1lb blackberries
2lb sugar (I used half granulated and have caster, as that's what I had in)
I'm not the best with measurements but I used about
2tbl spoons of lemon juice and 100ml water.

Cored and halved the plums and put them in the pan with the berries, lemon juice and water and then let it simmer for about 20 minutes. When all the fruit was soft I used the potato masher to break the berries down a bit more. I then use a sieve (and the trusty masher) so I can get about 1/3ish to half of the pulp out, otherwise I find there's just to many berry seeds in it.
Returned to the heat for a few minutes and then added the sugar - stirred until all dissolve and then brought back to the boil until I got the setting point which was about 15 minutes
Then I added about half a tablespoon of each of the spices and gave it a good mix, you can then put a bit on a plate to cool to see if you want to add more.

Plum Chutney by Tracey Colley.

1kg Plums, stoned and quartered
3 finely chopped onions
100g chopped sultanas
Couple of chopped cooking apples
Tbsp grated ginger
Tbsp black mustard seeds
Tbsp ground cumin
Tspn paprika
Tsp chilli flakes
750ml red wine vinegar
500g soft brown (light) sugar.

Put everything except sugar in pan and bring slowly to boil. Then simmer for 10 minutes. Add sugar and 2 tsp salt and boil uncovered for 20 - 30 minutes until thick and pulpy. Pot up and leave for about a month before using.

Potatoes

Spicy Potato Soup (With or without Chickpeas) by Helen Ruffles.

1 large onion chopped
Splash of oil, I used Rapeseed
Large knob of butter
1 tbsp curry powder
2 large potatoes, cubed 1 cm
400 ml milk
400 ml boiling water … you might need a bit more depending on thickness desired
1 stock cube (chicken or vegetable)
1 – 2 tsp mango chutney
Coriander to taste
Tin of rinsed chickpeas
Salt and pepper

Fry onions for about 5 minutes in oil and butter. Add curry powder and cook out for a couple of minutes. Add potatoes, stir and cook on low heat for about 10 minutes, covered. I added small amount of water to stop sticking. Add milk, water, stock cube and simmer until potatoes tender. Blitz. Add mango chutney, coriander and chickpeas (if using). Season to taste. Simmer for a few minutes.

Lithuanian Potato Pancakes (a bit like a hash brown) by Ieva Knell.

3 big potatoes (Jacket potato/baking potato size, floury ones are best)
1 egg
1/4 tsp of ground black pepper
1/2 tsp salt
oil for frying
Makes approx 8 palm size pancakes

Peel the potatoes and grate them on the fine side of the grater. Add salt and pepper. Add egg and mix through very well until egg is properly incorporated in the mixture, you don't want little blobs of unmixed egg (I just use a fork and do a bit of whisking with it) . If the mixture is quite watery (it sort of depends on a type of potato and how fresh in the season they are) add about 1 tbsp of semolina or flour to soak up the liquid a bit. Heat up 2-3 tbsp of oil (I use sunflower oil) in a frying pan. Heavy carbon steel or cast iron pans are ideal for this but any pan will do. Add spoon-fulls of mixture to the pan to make palm sized pancakes (you can also make them small like blinis or fairly large), level a bit with the spoon and fry on medium high heat until edges start to colour and the bottom is the colour of caramel (golden brown), maybe 3 min per side depending on the size of the pancake. Turn, add a bit more oil if needed and cook until the bottom side of the pancake is golden brown. Best served hot while the outside is still crispy. I prefer mine with a generous dollop of sour cream, but creme fraiche or natural yogurt is also good. Hubby doesn't like any of these so he had it with BBQ sauce and declared it VERY good :) Good on it's own, or with a salad, or as a side dish or even with bacon and eggs.
Sometimes pancake mixture starts to turn slightly rusty colour then going grey, it's normal because when starch is exposed to oxygen it causes the potatoes to turn grey. If you don't like the colour then adding a teaspoon of lemon juice or a very small pinch of citric acid or crushing half a tablet of vitamin C and mixing it in can help the mixture from becoming too dark.

Potato and Swede Pasty by Pauline Lord.

FOR THE FILLING	FOR THE ROUGH PUFF PASTRY
225g potato	300g plain flour
125g swede	A pinch of sea salt
75g carrot	150g chilled unsalted butter, cut into small cubes

1 small onion, grated
A handful of parsley, finely chopped
A few sprigs of thyme, leaves only, chopped
1 teaspoon vegetable bouillon powder
½ teaspoon freshly ground black pepper
½ teaspoon sea salt
50g strong Cheddar, grated (optional)
30g butter, melted

TO FINISH
1 egg, lightly beaten with
1 teaspoon milk, to glaze.

To make the pastry, mix the flour with the salt, then add the cubed butter and toss until the pieces are coated in the flour. Add just enough iced water (about 150ml) to bring the mixture together into a fairly firm dough. On a well-floured surface, shape the dough into a rectangle with your hands and then roll it out in one direction, away from you, so you end up with a rectangle about 1cm thick. Fold the far third towards you, then fold the nearest third over that (rather like folding a business letter), so that you now have a rectangle made up of 3 equal layers. Give the pastry a quarter turn, then repeat the rolling, folding and turning process 5 more times. Wrap the pastry in cling film and rest in the fridge for about 30 minutes, up to an hour.

Preheat the oven to 190°C. For the filling, peel the potato, swede and carrot and cut into 3–4mm dice. Mix together with all the other ingredients in a bowl, adding the butter last of all to bind.

Roll out the pastry on a lightly floured surface to approximately a 3mm thickness. Using a 19cm plate as a template, cut out 4 circles; you may have to gather up the trimmings then re-roll them to get your fourth circle.

Spoon the vegetable mixture on to one half of each circle. Brush the pastry edges with a little water, fold the other half of the pastry over the filling to form a half-moon shape and crimp the edges well to seal.

Place the pasties on a baking sheet lined with baking parchment and brush with the egg glaze. Bake for about 35–40 minutes, until the pastry is golden brown. Eat hot or cold.

Pumpkins

Pumpkin Pie by Caroline Perley. (Carla Boyd's Mom xx)

1 cup sugar
1 tsp ginger
½ tsp of each (salt, allspice, cloves, nutmeg),
1 ½ tsp cinnamon,
2 large or 3 small eggs,
1 7/8 cups of evaporated milk (465 ml),
1 ½ cups prepared pumpkin.

Mix all ingredients until smooth, place in unbaked pie shell, bake first at 425F for 15 minutes then bake at 350F for about 35-40 minutes until baked (insert toothpick should come out clean). Then let cool on top of stove before serving with ice cream or whipped cream.

Prepared pumpkin - cut up pumpkin into small chunks. Add enough boiling water to cover pumpkin and cook on low over stove until pumpkin mushy and most of the water evaporates. Then strain the pumpkin rind out and the pumpkin left behind is thick non lumpy and creamy - like rice pudding.

Pie dough (Canadian style)2 cups strong white bread flour 1 cup lard (250 ml) 1 tsp salt and 1/2 cup water (125 ml) - mix together using a pastry cutter then add the water and mix together but not thoroughly Let sit under cover for 20 minutes divide into 4 portions and roll out on floury surface until 1/8 inch thick (not too thin please!) place in bottom of pie tin and cut around edges of tin to trim. Can also be used for flaky Apple pie pastry crust as well (too be honest - the standard pie crust in Canada !)

Pumpkin Pie by Jackie Hughes.

450g Pumpkin
200g Short-crust pastry.
2 Eggs Beaten
100g caster sugar
60ml Milk
pinch ground nutmeg
pinch ground ginger
10ml ground cinnamon

Cut the pumpkin into pieces, remove any seeds and cotton-woolly
inside part and cut off the outside skin. Steam the pieces of pumpkin
between 2 plates over a pan of boiling water until tender- 15 or so
minutes- and drain thoroughly. Mash well with a fork or puree in an
electric blender.

Roll out the pastry and use it to line a 20.5cm flan case or deep pie
plate; trim and decorate the edges. Beat the eggs with the sugar. Add
the pumpkin, milk and spices. Blend well and pour into the pastry
case. Bake in the oven at 220C for 15 minutes, then reduce the
temperature to 180 and bake for a further 30 minutes or until the
filling is set. Serve warm with cream.

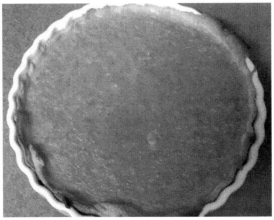

Image by Jackie Hughes, Pumpkin Pie.

Pumpkin and Carrot Thai Soup by Tracy Goree.

Pumpkin
Carrots
Small-medium sized sweet potato
1 Onion
1 clove garlic
Grated fresh ginger (about 2 teaspoons)
Oil for cooking
Fresh or dried chilli
Zest of 1 lime
Tin of coconut milk
Curry powder to personal taste
Vegetable stock
Coriander - a bunch

Chop everything up. Fry off the onion until softened. Add the garlic, chilli and ginger. Cook and stir a minute or 2. Add curry powder. Stir in for about 1 minute. Add remaining ingredients, except coconut milk, plus stock. Use enough stock to just cover everything.

Bring to boil and then simmer until everything is cooked. Add coriander, stalks and all. Liquidise, then add coconut milk. Return to the boil, then simmer for about 10 minutes. You may need to stir every couple of minutes to stop it from catching on the bottom of the pan.

Apologies if this is rather basic but I rarely weigh anything!!

Pumpkin Bread by Lesley Peachey's Allotment Neighbour!

19oz Pumpkin Pulp
13 oz Granulated Sugar
7 ½ oz Raisins
8 flo oz Corn Oil
4 Eggs
6 ½ oz Strong white bread flour
6 ½ oz Strong brown bread flour
2 tsp Baking Powder
1 ½ tsp bicarbonate of Soda
3 tsp Cinnamon Powder
1 tsp salt
(Chopped nuts can be added as well, type and amount to taste)

Prepare the Pumpkin
Cut up the pumpkin into chunks and take out the seeds. Place the pumpkin pieces in a large dish with a little drop of water in the bottom and cook at 180C until tender, leave to cool. Scrap all the pumpkin flesh off the skin, mash well and place in a colander: leave to drain over night. Divide into 19oz portions, these can be frozen and then are ready to use at any time of the year.

Pre-heat the over to 180c (350F or gas mark 4) Line two 2lb load tins. Mix together the flour, baking powder, soda, cinnamon and salt. Mix together the pumpkin pulp, sugar, raisins, oil and eggs in a large bowl. Gradually stir the dry ingredients into the mixture. Divide the mixture between the two tins and bake for about 1 hour.

Pumpkin Chutney by Jayne Hickling.

3lb Pumpkin (Emptied, peeled, deseeded and cubed)
3lb Apples
1lb Onions
3/4 lb Sultanas (optional)
1 1/2 Pint Vinegar
1lb Sugar
2 tsp Ground Ginger
1tsp Pepper
1 tsp Ground Cloves
1 tsp Cayenne

Finely chop and mince all of the ingredients together. Put into a large
saucepan with the vinegar and spices and cook until softened and
slightly reduced, then add the sugar. Continue cooking until
thickened.
Makes about 20 jars of chutney! The last time I made this I didn't use
Cayenne- because I didn't have any.... it was a mild and nicely sweet
chutney. Have now made it with the Cayenne.... that's some hot
spicy chutney...... nice- but hoping the heat calms down a bit!!!! Fine
for some of the chilli heads!!!

R
Radishes

Spicy Quick Pickled Radishes by Karen Parry.

1 bunch radishes
175ml white wine vinegar or apple cider vinegar
175ml water
3 ½ tablespoons honey or maple syrup
2 teaspoons salt
1 teaspoon red pepper flakes (this yields very spicy pickles, so use ½ teaspoon for medium spicy pickles or none at all)
½ teaspoon whole mustard seeds (optional)
Optional add-ins: garlic cloves, black peppercorns, fennel seeds, coriander seeds

To prepare the radishes: Slice off the tops and bottoms of the radishes, then use a sharp knife or mandolin to slice the radishes into very thin rounds. Pack the rounds into a pint-sized jar. Sprinkle over the top of the rounds with red pepper flakes and mustard seeds.
To prepare the brine: In a small saucepan, mix the vinegar, water, honey or maple syrup and salt. Bring the mixture to a boil, stirring occasionally and then pour the mixture over the radishes.
You need to let the mixture cool to room temperature. You can serve the pickles immediately or cover and refrigerate for later consumption. The pickles will keep well in the fridge for several weeks, although they are in their most fresh and crisp state for about 5 days after pickling. If you want to make it suitable for vegans you can swap the honey for maple syrup.

Red Cabbage

Pickled Red Cabbage by Jacqui Bones.

Approx 2 ½ lb red cabbage
4oz salt
1 ½ pints pickling vinegar

Remove any limp blemished outer leaves cut into ¼. Remove the hard core, slice the cabbage finely. Place in a bowl layering with salt cover and leave overnight. Next day drain and rinse cabbage pack fairly tightly in to clean jars cover completely with cold vinegar store for 7-10 days use quickly otherwise will go limp. Makes 4lb

Red Currants

Red Currant Shrub by Rebecca Willmott.

300ml of stained redcurrant juice,
600ml of rum or brandy,
finely grated zest of 1 orange,
1tsp grated nutmeg
300g granulated sugar.

Put all of the above except for the sugar in to a large wide necked jar
and store in a cool dark place for 10 - 14 days. After that, transfer
into a pan and add the sugar and warm to 60 degrees. When the
sugar has dissolved, strain through a jelly bag and decant into a
sterilised bottle and seal.

Red Currant Ice Cream by Gillian Young.

500g Redcurrants
100g granulated sugar- or to taste
300ml whipping cream

Pre-chill a plastic container in the freezer. Rinse the redcurrants in
water and pat dry. In a medium saucepan on a medium heat, cook the
redcurrants until the have burst. Strain the redcurrants through a fine
sieve and combine with sugar to taste. Chill in the fridge.

Whisk off the cream until stiff and fold into the redcurrant
concentrate. Pour into pre-chilled container, cover and freeze for 2
hours or until firm.

Raspberries

<u>Red Fruit Jelly by Jennifer Stead.</u>

1kg Redcurrants
1kg Raspberries
450ml water
Sugar
3tsp port

Put fruit in the pan with
water and simmer for 15-
20min until soft and pulpy.
Pour through jelly bag, leave
overnight. Add 450g sugar
for every 600ml juice. Warm
to dissolve, bring to the boil
for 9-10min until setting
point. Stir in port and then
pour into sterilised jars.

Image by Vanessa Brett Davey.

Rhubarb

Rhubarb Cake by Katrina Watson.

250g rhubarb cut into 1"
200g butter/ margarine
200g caster sugar
4eggs
150g Sr. Flour
50g ground almond
½ teaspoon vanilla essence

Cream sugar and butter add eggs, one at a time. Add flour, almonds and vanilla. Gently mix in rhubarb cook for 40 min at 180'c.

Rhubarb Chutney by Linda Ford.

1kg rhubarb
25g fresh ginger, well bruised (I put mine in a muslin square - makes it easier to remove at the end of cooking)
25g garlic, finely chopped
2 lemons (Grated rind as well as the juice)
1 tbs salt
2½ cups malt vinegar
1kg sugar (I use granulated)
500g mixed Raisins and Sultanas

Cut the rhubarb into small pieces. In a saucepan mix in the rhubarb with the ginger, garlic, grated rind and juice of the 2 lemons and the salt.
Add the vinegar and slowly bring to the boil, then add the sugar, raisins and sultanas. Boil very slowly until the mixture is thick, taking care that it doesn't burn. Remove the muslin bag with the ginger and keep going until it thickens- by doing the spoon test! Allow to cool, then spoon into clean jars and seal. Made about 3 litres.

Curried Rhubarb Chutney by Amy Patrick.

2lb Rhubarb
½ Sultanas (optional)
1oz Curry Powder, (can be more, depending on your own personal taste)
1 cup Malt Vinegar
2 Large Onions
2lb Sugar
1tbs Mustard Powder
½ tbls Salt

Chop the rhubarb into small chunks and chop the onion. Place all of the ingredients into a large preserving pan and cook slowly until everything is pulpy, which takes between 40 to 80 minutes. Jar up in sterilised jars, keep for around 3 months before tasting, so that the curry flavour has time to properly infuse and doesn't taste raw. Because I don't always use the sultanas I sometime add extra onion and a couple of extra stalks of rhubarb instead. Alternative Ingredients: Chilli, Ginger, Garlic, Dates, Apple Cider Vinegar, Pepper.

Image by Nan Roberts Massey, Rhubarb.

Rhubarb and Ginger Jam by Valerie Callen.

2 pounds 6 oz rhubarb,
2 dessert apples cored and chopped finely,
Juice of half a lemon plus rind of lemon grated
1 kilo of Jam sugar made 1.5 litres of jam.
(2.5 x 500 ml Kilner jars).

Rhubarb and apples layered with the sugar and left to extract juices overnight. No water added. Lessons learned, cut Rhubarb into one inch pieces, (I cut into 2 inch pieces and think smaller would have been better). Also, even if using jam sugar and juice of one lemon and grated lemon rind and the two small apples, best to add the all the pith of the squeezed half lemon and remove it immediately before jarring for a good firm set and exquisite flavour, brings out the ginger nicely but doesn't taste too "lemony". A spoonful of butter stirred in gives a nice glaze and helps eliminate bubbles of air when jarring. I used a 1.5 inch piece of root ginger grated, including skin, together with one level teaspoon of ground ginger. Take care when putting in jars, I found the inch rhubarb clumped together despite stirring before tipping out and it spilled down side of jar.

2

Image by Katrina Watson, Rhubarb Cake.

140

Rhubarb and Yoghurt Cake by Jacqui Bones.

200g rhubarb thinly chopped
310g SR flour
230g caster sugar
Zest 1 orange
2 eggs lightly beaten
125g plain yoghurt
125g unsalted butter melted
1tsp vanilla essence
1tbsp orange flower water
1tsp salt

Pre heat oven to 180c. Mix together rhubarb flour salt zest and sugar.
Mix together eggs yoghurt vanilla essence orange flower water and
melted and combine both mixtures but do not over mix. Pour into a
greased lined tin (round like a Christmas cake tin) level off. Bake for
25 minutes or until cooked through and golden (approx 45 minutes).
When cool serve with yoghurt and cream.

Roasted Rhubarb and Balsamic Vinegar Popsicles by Alison Renshaw.

To be made using a six hole ice-lolly mould and six sticks.
330g chopped sticks of Rhubarb
1 Vanilla Bean split sideways
1 Tablespoon Balsamic Glaze
1 Tablespoon Honey or Maple Syrup
400ml Coconut Milk
(90g extra maple syrup or honey)
80g Almonds, Chopped coarsely
Chocolate Coating
100g Virgin Coconut oil
2 Tablespoons cocoa powder
1 teaspoon vanilla extract
2 teaspoons maple syrup or honey.

Image by Alison Renshaw, Rhubarb Popsicles.

Preheat over to 200c. Line oven tray with baking paper. Place rhubarb and vanilla bean on the tray. Drizzle with balsamic vinegar and honey/ maple syrup. Roast for 15 minutes until tender. Cool and then remove the vanilla pod. Process or blend the rhubarb mixture with the coconut milk and extra honey/ maple syrup until smooth and pour into the moulds. Put in the stick and freeze for 4 hours.

When the ice-lollies are frozen, make the chocolate coating. Line an over tray with baking paper and place in the freezer. Pour the chocolate coating into a small, deep bowl. Place nuts in another small bowl. Briefly dip the ice-lollies into boiling water. Next dip them straight into the chocolate followed by the nuts. Place onto the cold tray and then put back into the freezer for 5 minutes or until the coating is set.

Chocolate coating: Place the oil, sifted cocoa powder, extract and honey/ maple syrup into a saucepan over a low heat. Stir until the oil is melted and the mixture is combined. Remove from heat and stand at room temperature until cool.

Rhubarb and Orange Marmalade by Kate Gibbs.

750g rhubarb, chopped
1.2kg sugar
2 medium oranges (quartered and seeds removed)

Mix the chopped rhubarb and sugar in a large heavy saucepan. Chop oranges, including the peels, in a food processor; add to rhubarb mixture. Bring to the boil. Reduce heat and simmer, uncovered, stirring often until marmalade starts to set, usually between 1 and 2 hours.
Pour into clean jam jars that have been sterilised in your dishwasher or oven. Cover securely with tight fitting lids and store in a dark place.

Rhubarb and Vanilla Jam by Jayne Hickling.

2lb rhubarb, chopped into small pieces
2 vanilla pods
2lb preserving sugar
5 tbsp apple pectin (or two small apples!)

Put all of the ingredients in a pan with 150ml water and simmer until the rhubarb starts to soften. Once setting point has been reached, using the drag and trail method, take out the vanilla pods. Pour the hot jam into sterilised jam jars and screw on the lids whilst still hot.

Rhubarb Cake by Ann Marie.

300g rhubarb
Juice of ½ a lemon
165g self-raising flour
175g butter softened, plus extra for greasing
175g caster sugar
3 large eggs
2 tsp vanilla extract
For the topping
25g unsalted butter
2tbsp self-raising flour
2tbsp caster sugar
2tsp ground ginger

Preheat the oven to 180c. Grease and line 23cm loaf tin. Prepare the rhubarb and cut into 3cm pieces and put in a bowl with the lemon juice. Beat flour, sugar, eggs, butter and vanilla extract. Fold in half of the rhubarb and spoon into the bottom of the tin. Scatter the other half of the rhubarb over the top. Rub the butter into the flour and then stir in the sugar and ginger. You then need to sprinkle over the top of cake mix, like a rhubarb crumble, and bake for 40-50mins.

Easy Peasy Rhubarb Jelly by Caz Sumner.

5 Sticks of Rhubard (Chopped into chunks)
Strawberry Jelly

Cook the rhubarb in the microwave for about 5 minutes. You don't need to add any water at all. Get the jelly. I use the powdered version but you can use the blocks of jelly they both work exactly the same. On the powdered jelly- ... Ignore the instructions on the back! Use just 1 sachet. Add 100ml of boiling water to the powder and stir. Add jelly to stewed rhubarb. At this point check if you need to add sugar... My rhubarb is lovely and sweet this year so I don't add any I like it slightly tangy. Blitz to make it smooth and add some air to the jelly. Put into pots. I finish mine off with a dollop of custard but you can have it plain. Leave to set in the fridge for a few hours then tuck in!

Rhubarb Bitters by Stephen Baird.

About 1lb of rhubarb stalk chopped into 1" lengths (try for young thin stalks)
1 bottle of over proof white spirit (vodka or rum is best)
Rind of 1 1/2 large oranges (ensure as much pith is gone as possible)
1 heaped tbs dried juniper berries
1 heaped tbs coriander seeds
Good tbs of dried Cassia Bark

Put all into large kilner jar and give a good shake when closed. Let steep for about 14 days, giving a shake every day. After this time strain out the solids and put the liquid in a jar, then add a mug of water to the solids and heat gently for about 5 minutes, let it cool. Put in the jar with the other liquid then let steep for another 2 days. Strain through a sieve (or cheesecloth) getting out as much liquid as possible then bottle, keeps well as the alcohol content is really high.

Rhubarb, Apple and Cinnamon Crumble by Jayne Hickling.

Filling:
10 Sticks Rhubarb
2 Cooking Apples
3 Dessert Spoons Caster Sugar
2 teaspoons ground cinnamon
Crumble:
4 oz Margarine/ butter
4oz Caster Sugar
8 oz Plain Flour

Cut the Rhubarb into 5cm chunks and put into a baking dish. Mix in chopped apples and then sprinkle with the sugar and cinnamon and 2 dessert spoons of water. Put the dish into the oven for 10 minutes at 190c. Make up the crumble topping by mixing all of the ingredients together and forming a crumb mixture. Take the filling out of the oven and give it a good stir and then top with the crumble. Either freeze at this point (once the filling has cooled) or put it back into the oven for another 15 minutes, until the crumble is browned.

Spiced Rhubarb with Ginger Chutney by Jacqui Bones.

2lb trimmed rhubarb
½ pint pickling vinegar
1lb white sugar
8 cloves
½ level tsp ground ginger
2-3 pieces of stem ginger chopped

Wash the rhubarb dry and cut into 1 inch lengths put the vinegar sugar cloves and ginger in a pan. Heat gently until sugar dissolves then bring to boil and boil for 5 minutes. Add the rhubarb bring back to the boil and simmer until the rhubarb is tender but keeping its shape. Leave until cold. Drain off juice boil hard until thick and syrupy. Mix rhubarb and ginger together pack into warm sterilised jars seal. Store for a week before use. Makes approx 2lb.

Rhubarb and Orange Jam by Chris Murray.

1kg of rhubarb,
3 tblsp of orange juice and the zest of 1 orange,
300ml of water
1.3kg of jam sugar.

Add the water, rhubarb, orange juice and zest.... simmer until the rhubarb if soft and the mixture is reduced by half. Then add the jam sugar making sure it's dissolved and rapidly boil for 10 minutes.

<u>Spicy Rhubarb and Apple Chutney by Helen Ruffles.</u>

Approx 850 g Rhubarb, chopped (had been frozen and thawed)
4 large Bramley Apples, peeled and chopped
2 large red onions, finely chopped
8 large garlic cloves finely sliced
Few chilli flakes or finely chopped chilli
Thumb sized piece of fresh ginger, grated
2 or 3 Star Anise
2 tsp cinnamon or cinnamon sticks
1 tsp cumin seeds
Just under tbsp salt
250mls white wine vinegar
500 g caster sugar

Put all ingredients into pan except sugar and rhubarb. Bring to boil,
turn down heat, cover and simmer for about 30 minutes until the
apples are pulpy. Add Rhubarb and sugar. Bring to boil and leave to
bubble away for about 40 minutes, just stirring occasionally.
Carefully take out the star anise and cinnamon stick. Put straight into
sterilised jars. Leave for at least a month for vinegar to mellow,
although because this is white wine vinegar, it shouldn't take as long
as a malt vinegar would!!! Will keep at least a year in properly
sterilised jars.

Rhubarb Gin by Debs Webster.

400g chopped rhubarb,
50g sugar,
Splash lemon juice.
70cl Gin

Put in jar and shake. Add 70cl gin. Shake every day for 2 weeks.
Strain. Sweeten if you want with 70g + 35ml water (make a syrup
first) you may not need it all. .....chill and drink. Use pink bits of
rhubarb.

Rhubarb Vodka by Debs Webster.

1 litre vodka
2 sticks rhubarb
zest of half a lemon
3 cloves
1 cinnamon stick
3 tbsp sugar

This does take about 3 months to be ready, so you have to be
patient!!! Bash the rhubarb and put in a jar with sugar, leave for 2
days to steep. After 2 days, add the rest of ingredients and shake
daily for 3 weeks, strain and put in clean jar/bottle, leave for 3
months before drinking.

Rhubarb and Ginger Muffins by Celia Stapleton.

400 g of self raising flour (or 3 teaspoons of baking powder with plain flour)
1 teaspoon salt
125 mls oil (sunflower or whatever you prefer)
250 mls milk
200 g sugar
2 eggs

You can use this mix and add all sorts of things to it -grated orange or lemon peel with sultanas, banana and chocolate chips etc
For the rhubarb muffins I sometimes substitute two tablespoonfuls of the flour for same of oats, added two teaspoonfuls of ground ginger and chopped. One large stick of rhubarb by cutting it lengthways and then into short pieces to make cubes. I prefer them smaller in cake cases not muffin cases, medium oven about 20 minutes or until risen and light brown on top.

Image by Celia Stapleton, Rhubarb and Ginger Muffins.

Rosehips

Rosehip Syrup by Cid Eric.

1kg Rosehips
750gr Sugar
Water

Any rosehips I de-stalk about 1kg of hips blitz them in batches with a little water in a blender put them all in a pan with about 1 Ltr of water bring to the boil for a few min then switch off the heat and let them sit for 15 min strain through Muslin, put hips back in pan and add some more water to make your liquid up to about a Ltr again repeat heating straining when you have enough add 750gr sugar and bring to the boil switch off and put into sterilised bottles . Job done. Awesome on ice cream pancakes or as a cordial.

Image by Cid Eric, Rosehip Syrup.

Runner Beans

Runner Bean and Courgette Chutney by Jane Scrivens.

1lb runner beans, thinly sliced
4 courgettes, thinly sliced
10oz cooking apples, peeled, cored and finely chopped
2 onions, finely chopped
1lb light soft brown sugar
1tsp mustard powder
1tsp turmeric
1tsp coriander seeds
1pt white wine vinegar

Put the beans, courgettes, apples and onions in a preserving pan, then add the sugar, mustard powder, turmeric and coriander seeds. Pour in the vinegar and stir. Cook over a gentle heat, stirring until all the sugar has dissolved. Bring to the boil and cook at a rolling boil , stirring occasionally, for about 10 minutes. Reduce to a simmer and cook for about 1 ½ hours, stirring from time to time, until the mixture thickens. Stir constantly near the end of the cooking time so that the mixture does not stick to the bottom of the pan. Pot and cover in the usual way. Store in a cool dark place. Allow flavours to mature for one month before using and refrigerate after opening.

S
Saffron

Saffron and Cardamom Buns by Kate Wood.

300 ml milk
large pinch of saffron
3 tablespoons honey
1 teaspoon vanilla
Cardamom seeds from 20 or so pods (about 2 T cardamom seeds)
30 grams butter
500 grams strong white flour
1 tsp salt
1 tsp yeast
1 egg yolk
Pearl sugar or Demerara sugar

These are Scandinavian-inspired, though I didn't follow a specific recipe. They're reminiscent of Finnish Pulla or Coffee Bread, but less work! Combine the milk, cardamom, and saffron in a small pan. Heat on medium heat until the milk is steaming. Let cool for about 20 minutes and add the butter, honey and vanilla. If using a bread machine, combine the rest of the ingredients and use your sweet dough setting (or white dough setting if none). If doing by hand, stir the yeast into the cooled milk mixture. Then add the flour and salt, knead and let rise.

After the first rise or end of the dough cycle, punch down and let rest . Divide up into 12 balls (should be about 75 grams each). Form into rolls and put in a greased baking pan. Let rise until 1 1/2 times original size. (This is a sweet dough so it'll be a slow rise, allow an hour but check after 45 minutes.) Pre-heat oven to 200 (190 fan). Brush with an egg yolk wash and sprinkle with pearl or Demerara sugar. Bake 10 minutes uncovered, then cover with aluminium foil for another 10 minutes of bake time.

Saffron Cake by Suzan Brett.

1 tsp saffron strands
125ml milk
500g plain flour, plus extra for dusting
½ tsp dried, fast-action yeast
pinch salt
¼ tsp freshly grated nutmeg
250g cold butter, cut into cubes, plus extra for greasing
250g caster sugar
300g currants
50g candied peel
clotted cream, to serve

Grease a 1kg loaf tin with butter. Heat the saffron strands and milk in a pan over a medium heat until the milk mixture has turned yellow and is almost simmering. In a separate bowl, mix together the flour, yeast, salt and nutmeg. You then need to add the butter and sugar, whilst rubbing in using your fingertips until the mixture is bread crumbed. Stir in the currants and candied peel. Pour over the saffron-infused milk and stir until the mixture comes together as a soft dough. Take the dough out of the bowl onto a lightly floured work surface and knead lightly until smooth. Put the dough into the prepared loaf tin. Cover with a damp tea towel, in a warm place for about 30-45 minutes, until risen.

Preheat the oven to 180C. Put the saffron cake to the oven and bake for 45 minutes to one hour, or until the cake is pale golden-brown and has risen. Let the cake cool slightly, before taking it out of the loaf tin, onto a plate and cut into slices.

Shallots

Pickled Shallots by Natasha Garner.

Shallots
Salt water
Malt Vinegar
Cider Vinegar
tsp whole cloves
tsp mustard seeds
tsp peppercorns
bay leaves

I put mine in boiling water, for a few minutes then drained and ran them under cold water, top and tailed and removed the skin easily. Made up a solution of salt water and soaked for 24 hours. Sterilised my jars, added a large jar of malt vinegar, a bit of cider vinegar, a tsp whole cloves, tsp mustard seeds, tsp peppercorns, few bay leaves to a pan and brought to boil then turned off cooled completely. Fill jars to brim, add vinegar and lid. Store in dark place for at least a month ideally 6-8 weeks.

Sloe Berries

Sloe and Apple Jelly by Mary Fothergill.

450g Sloes, (roughly quartered with peel and core intact)
450g Cooking Apple, (roughly quartered with peel and core intact)
Water to cover
Granulated Sugar- as required
450g to 600ml Apple juice.

Mince or process the fruit, then cook very slowly in the water until soft but not pulpy. Test for pectin and boil for a little longer if necessary. Line a sieve with a piece of clean, fine cloth and place it over a heatproof bowl large enough to hold the contents of the pan. (Alternatively use a jelly bag). Pour boiling water through the cloth to scald it and empty the water out of the bowl and discard. Pour the cooked fruit into the cloth and allow to drain. (The bag can be suspended to increase the flow). Measure the juice and weigh out the appropriate amount of sugar. Pour the juice into a large saucepan and add the sugar. Dissolve over a low heat, stirring gently, and then boil rapidly until setting point is reached. Pot and seal immediately in sterilised jars.

Image by Mary Fothergill, Foraged Sloe Berries.

Strawberries

Strawberry and Rhubarb Jam by Lesley Rayner.

1lb rhubarb
1lb strawbs
2lb sugar
Juice of 1 lemon

Cook as normal for jam until setting point reached, it's that easy

Strawberry Sorbet by Phillipa Clarke.

450g ripe strawberries,
hulled and chopped.
100g caster sugar.
1 pinch salt.
1 ½ teaspoons of cornflour.
1 ½ teaspoons cold water
3 tablespoons of lemon juice.

Put strawberries in food processor until smooth. Combine sugar salt and pureed fruit in saucepan and heat until sugar has melted. Whisk cornflour in cold water and add to simmering mixture. Leave to cool for a couple of hours before freezing in an ice-cream maker according to manufacturers instructions.

Image by Amanda Whatley, Mixed Berry Jam.

Strawberry Pavlova by Anne Wriglesworth.

It's so easy, but next time I make it I will make smaller ones and freeze them before adding the fruit and cream.

4 egg whites
7oz Caster Sugar
1tsp Cornflour
1tsp Vanilla Essence
1tsp White wine Vinegar
300ml Double Cream
2tbs Icing Sugar
14oz Strawberries (or mixed fruit)

You line a baking sheet with baking parchment and mark out a 7-8in circle in the middle. Then whisk the egg whites to stiff peaks, whisk 4 tbsp of caster sugar taken from 7oz (1 at a time) make sure it stiffens again. Fold in the remaining sugar. Add the cornflour, same vanilla essence, and white wine vinegar and whisk until mixed in well. Pile the meringue into the baking sheet, and make a dip in the middle for the cream and fruit. Bake for about 1 hr, or until it's firm to touch and you can peel off the parchment, at 140C. Leave to cool. Whisk the double cream with the icing sugar, pile it in the middle of the Pavlova and add strawberries or mixed fruits which have been washed and dried. Enjoy!!!(It's lovely as it has a soft centre).

Strawberry and Prosecco Jam by Jenny Blake.

150ml Prosecco
1kg Jam Sugar
1kg Strawberries

Put the Prosecco, Jam Sugar and strawberries into a large heavy-based saucepan and place over a low heat, stirring until the sugar has dissolved. Increase the heat and boil steadily for 10 minutes, taking care to keep an eye on the jam to ensure that it doesn't boil too rapidly. Test the jam for setting point. If this point has not been reached, return the saucepan to the heat and continue to boil for another 2 minutes. Test as before until setting point is reached. (You may need to test several times). Pour the hot jam into the warm sterilized jars. Leave to cool.

Fool Proof Strawberry Jam by Steven Moseley.

1 kg strawberries
1 kg jam sugar.
Knob of butter
Splash of lemon juice.

I freeze my strawberries and then put them in the pot frozen. Warm them up and keep stirring till defrosted and soft. Give them a good mashing and heat through on a medium heat for around 10 minutes then put in the sugar butter and juice. Stir and heat until all sugar has dissolved and then turn up the heat a little. Allow to come to a rolling boil and let it boil for 5 minutes. Test a bit on a plate that has been in the freezer. It should skin over within a few seconds. If it does then turn off heat and jar up. If not, keep boiling and testing every minute.

Strawberry Vinegar by Jacqui Bones.

450g raspberries
600ml white wine vinegar
225g sugar

I made strawberry vinegar as a salad dressing. Just change the
strawberries to raspberries for a change, never tried gooseberries. I
put into small bottles is sweeter than the raspberry one. Can also use
Damsons. Allow 600ml/1 pint white wine vinegar to each 450g/1 lb
raspberries.
Crush the fruit in a large bowl and pour the vinegar over.
Then leave to steep for 3 days, stirring often. Strain through a
muslin-lined sieve into a large measuring jug. Add 225g/8 oz sugar
to each pint of juice in a pan and heat to boiling. Boil for 10 minutes
and then pour into sterilised jars and seal tightly
Keep the vinegar out of direct sunlight and use within one year.

Strawberry and Rhubarb Pie by Kate Wood.

500ml Strawberries
500ml Rhubarb
200 ml Sugar
2 teaspoons corn-flour
Pinch of cinnamon
Shortcrust pastry

Chop up equal amounts of strawberries and rhubarb, about 500ml
each. Mix together and add about 200ml sugar, a couple teaspoons of
cornflour, and a bit of cinnamon, and stir together. Put in a pie tin
and cover with regular or sweet shortcrust pastry. I like to cut mine
in a lattice pattern, it's pretty, but you don't have to. Bake at about
175c for 45 minutes or so until golden brown and bubbly. Let cool
completely before eating. Nice with vanilla ice cream!

Sweet Potato

Sweet Potato and Red Pepper Soup by Nan Roberts Massey.

2 Red Peppers
1 Sweet Potato
1 Red Onion
1 vegetable stock cube.
One pint water.

Chop vegetables and put in hot oven till pepper skin starts to go black. Leave to cool. Try to peel as much skin from pepper. Put all vegetables in pan with pint vegetable stock. Boil then blend.

Sweetcorn

Sweetcorn Chowder by Janet Gibson.

1 Onion
1 Potato
Three Corn Cobs
Parsley
Vegetable or Chicken Stock
1 Tbsp. Cream

Sweat off onions and add diced potatoes. Remove all corn from cob and add that to the pot. Add vegetable or chicken stock then simmer. Finish with a handful of chopped parsley and a dollop of cream. Do it in any quantities to your taste...comes out delicious every time. Season to taste and enjoy. Freezes well too!!

Image by Janet Gibson, Sweetcorn Chowder.

Chinese Style Sweetcorn Soup by Jayne Hickling.

3 large Corn on the Cobs
(or one can creamed
sweetcorn and one can
plain corn)
1 pint of water
Vegetable Stock Cube
1 tsp Chinese Five Spice
1 tsp Ground Ginger
1 tsp Ground Coriander
1 Egg White
1 tsp oil
1 tsp cornflour

Image by Jayne Hickling, Chinese Style Sweetcorn Soup.

Boil the three cobs in water until cooked- strain, but keep the
cooking liquid. Remove the corn from two of the cobs by running a
knife down the cobs into a bowl. Take two tablespoons of the
cooking fluid and the corn from the two cobs and blitz into creamed
sweetcorn. In another saucepan, put in the pint of water and bring to
the boil to dissolve the vegetable stock cube. Add the spices
followed by the creamed sweetcorn. Remove the corn from the third
cob and add to the pan. Bring to the boil. Mix the cornflour with a
little water to make a paste. Add to the soup to thicken. Once
thickened, in a separate bowl, mix the egg white with the tsp of oil.
Then add the egg mixture to the soup, stirring continually whilst you
do this to create string cooked egg white in the soup.
You could easily turn this into chicken and sweetcorn soup or crab
meat and sweetcorn soup by adding the cooked proteins at the same
point as the whole corn kernels. You could also use chicken stock
instead of vegetable stock. Finally you could also add sliced spring
onions at the same time as the corn.

T
Tomatillos

Salsa de Tomatillos by Jackie Hughes.

10 tomatillos, husked
1 small onion chopped
3 cloves garlic,chopped
2 jalapeño peppers chopped
Quarter cup of coriander fresh chopped
Salt and pepper to taste

Place tomatillos in a non reactive pan with enough water to cover. Bring to boil, simmer until tomatillo soften and begin to burst about ten minutes. Drain tomatillo s and place in blender with all other ingredients, salt and pepper to taste. Blend to desired consistency. I took seeds out of peppers but still hot enough for me!!

Image by Anne Morris, Green Tomato Chutney.

Tomatoes

Green Tomato Chutney by Jacqui Bones.

1lb green tomatoes
¾ lb cooking apples
½ lb peeled onions
2 cloves garlic crushed
1 ½ tsp salt
¾ pt pickling vinegar
4oz sultanas
2 tsp freshly grated ginger or ground ginger
10oz Demerara sugar

Chop tomatoes apples onions place in a large pan with all the other ingredients other than the sugar. Bring to the boil and simmer for 20 minutes or until soft. Stir in the sugar until dissolved then simmer uncovered until thick and no excess liquid. Pour in to sterilised jars label store for at least week.

Tomato Sauce by Alice Duckworth.

Using a mixture of sungold large cherry toms, tigerella and plum toms.
Onions
Garlic
Beef stock (vegetable stock if needed instead)

Simply slow roast the tomatoes at 150c for an hour then add to softened onion, garlic and beef stock. Blitzed with a hand blender and seasoned. Nothing else added!!!!!!

Tomato sauce by Jacqui Bones.

1.8 kg tomatoes sliced
100g onions sliced.
1 pepper chopped
2-3 chillies chopped
6 garlic crushed
15g salt
Szechuan pepper good pinch
175g sugar
225g apples chopped
450ml vinegar spiced
1tsp of each ground cinnamon ground cayenne pepper ground allspice

Put apples tomatoes onions pepper chillies and garlic in a pan simmer add spiced continue to simmer until all the pulp has been released at this point either strain or liquidise to a smooth liquid. Return to the pan with sugar and vinegar boil for 5minutes and bottle.

Image by Jacqui Bones, Tomato Sauce.

Red Tomato Pickle by Jacqui Bones.

2lb red tomatoes
3oz salt
1 pint water
¾ pickling vinegar
1 clove garlic
¾ lb white sugar

Peel the tomatoes by plunging in boiling water for about 20 seconds.
Then into cold water skins will split and slide off. Cut into thick
slices about 4 per tomato. Dissolve salt in cold water add tomatoes
leave to soak for 2-3 hours rinse off excess salt in cold water then
drain well. Put vinegar and garlic into a pan with the sugar heat
gently until sugar dissolves bring to the boil add tomatoes bring back
to the boil simmer for 2 minutes. Carefully pack the tomatoes into
warm jars boil the vinegar until it begins to thicken strain and pour
over the tomatoes to fill the jars. Seal store for 1-2 weeks.

Tomato Pasta Sauce by Hazel Turner.

Whole tomatoes chopped in half
5 small garlic put through a press
Large teaspoon of chopped chillies
Oregano and Basil a good sprinkle
1 Large onion chopped

The amount of tomatoes I used filled a large saucepan, sorry I did
not weigh them . Just put everything into saucepan and cook on
simmer for about ½ an hour. Then use a stick blender to make a
smoother sauce, but not to smooth. Cool and freeze into portions.

Tomato, Ginger and Chilli Chutney by Alison Bull.

500g Onions, Chopped
1.5kg Tomatoes
400g Granulated Sugar
250ml Cider Vinegar
50g Fresh Ginger, Sliced and chopped
½ Cinnamon Stick
1-2tsp Chilli Flakes
½ tsp Salt

Simmer tomatoes and onions for an hour until much of the liquid has been driven off. Add other ingredients and boil, stirring all of the time until you leave a trail for a second or two with the spoon. Put in warmed jars (4 or 5 medium ones) and keep for one month before opening.

Chunky Tomato Relish by Mary Fothergill.

1 tablespoons Olive Oil
1 Small Brown Onion
2 Cloves Garlic
1 Chilli
500g Tomatoes- Chopped
2 Tablespoons Brown Sugar
2 Tablespoons White Wine Vinegar

Heat oil in a pan, add the onions until soft. Add Garlic, Chilli and cook for two minutes. Add tomatoes to onion mix for five minutes. Add sugar and vinegar and cook until it thickens.

Tomato Preserve by Valentyna Kryvokon.

1.5 kg of ripe tomatoes
1.5ltr of water for marinade
3tb spoons of sugar
2tb spoons of salt
3-5tb spoons of white vinegar
leaves of black currant,
leaves of horseradish,
garlic, green dill, pepper, green parsley or celery

I firmly stack the tomatoes into clean jars. On each layer of tomatoes I put green leaves of black currant, leaves of horseradish, garlic, green dill, pepper, green parsley or celery. Then I pour the tomatoes up to the top with boiling water, pour carefully, not to burst the jar. Then stand so for 15 minutes. Meanwhile I do the marinade: boiling water , pepper , salt , sugar , vinegar. I pour out that water into the sink and pour marinade into the same jar. I close the jar with hot lid turn it upside down and cover with a blanket. After 12 hours, I put them on the bottom.

Tomato Soup or Sauce by Debs Webster.

2lb red tomatoes,
1 onion (chopped)
2 carrots (diced)
2 cups chicken stock.

Cook onions in a pan with a little butter for 5 minutes, add Tom's, carrots, stock, season and cover and simmer for 15/20 minutes. Whizz up and sieve. Add cream if you want a creamy soup/ sauce. If you want it as a sauce, thicken slightly and add some fresh chopped Tom's and basil. Great with tomato or spinach pasta xx

Spicy Tomato Relish by Linda Phillips.

4lb ripe plum tomatoes skinned and chopped
2lb 4oz Onions, chopped
1 garlic clove, crushed
½ tsp chilli flakes
1 tsp mustard seeds
1 tsp ground Ginger
1tbsp Chilli powder
1 tsp salt
1lb 10oz Caster Sugar
3 ½ oz Light Brown Soft Sugar
16fl oz Malt Vinegar
Salt to taste

Put all of the ingredients except the sugars, vinegar and salt into a large pan. Bring slowly to the boil and simmer gently, uncovered, for 1 hour, until thick. Add the sugars and vinegar and cook for 20 minutes. Add salt to taste. Allow to cool briefly before pouring into warm sterilised jars with rubber- lined or plastic lids then seal, cool and label. The relish can be eaten the next day or stored, sealed, for up to 6 months. Once open, refrigerate and eat within a week.

V

Vine Leaves

Stuffed Vine Leaves by Julie Reppe.

These are approximate as I eyeball it..... I love lemon juice so I use lots...
but it's depending on taste
Vine leaves
500g mince (beef or lamb)
½ teaspoon cinnamon
½ teaspoon mixed spice
Juice of 1-2 lemons. (Again I use lots but depends on taste..)
½ cup rice
1 tin chopped tomatoes
2 cloves of crushed garlic (not traditional... And optional)
1 tablespoon tomato purée
1 tablespoon mint (I use much more. Again to taste)
½ teaspoon mixed herbs.

Mix everything but the water tomato purée and water together, (keep the
tin) spread out a vine leaf (put any ripped or small leaves to one side) and
place a small amount of meat on it.. If the mix feels very wet squeeze a
little out, but you do need some moisture in it or will be very dry when
cooked. Fold the leaf over the meat as if wrapping a parcel, and then roll
up. Its a bit hard to explain, but I'm sure you can find a bid on YouTube if
your stuck..
Place the stuffed leaves in a large pan. Fill the tomato tin with water
making sure to get any traces of tomato ... Mix in the purée and add to your
vine leaves to just cover them.. Then place the ripped/small leaves on top
and cover with a lid... Bring to the boil and simmer at a low heat until the
meat is cooked and rice is tender... 30-40 minutes depending on the amount
of stuffed leaves in the pan...
If you can't get vine leaves, cabbage leaves will work but don't taste as
good, this mix can also be stuffed in to bell peppers.

W
White Cabbage

Coleslaw by Jayne Hickling.

1 White Cabbage- Shredded
1 Brown Onion- Grated
3 Carrots- Grated
1 Apple- Grated
5 Tablespoons of Mayonnaise

Shred the cabbage and put into a bowl, next grate in the onion, carrots and apple. Mix together. Finally, add the mayonnaise and fold into the whole mixture. You could also add grated beetroot. For a slightly fruity alternative, add some pineapple chucks- but only when you're ready to serve, as it may separate the mayonnaise if kept in the fridge for later use.

Weights and Conversion Tables

Weights of common ingredients in grams							
Ingredient	1 cup	3/4 cup	2/3 cup	1/2 cup	1/3 cup	1/4 cup	2 Tbsp
Flour, all purpose (wheat)	120 g	90 g	80 g	60 g	40 g	30 g	15 g
Flour, well sifted all purpose (wheat)	110 g	80 g	70 g	55 g	35 g	27 g	13 g
Sugar, granulated cane	200 g	150 g	130 g	100 g	65 g	50 g	25 g
Confectioner's sugar (cane)	100 g	75 g	70 g	50 g	35 g	25 g	13 g
Brown sugar, packed firmly (but not too firmly)	180 g	135 g	120 g	90 g	60 g	45 g	23 g
Corn meal	160 g	120 g	100 g	80 g	50 g	40 g	20 g
Corn starch	120 g	90 g	80 g	60 g	40 g	30 g	15 g
Rice, uncooked	190 g	140 g	125 g	95 g	65 g	48 g	24 g
Macaroni, uncooked	140 g	100 g	90 g	70 g	45 g	35 g	17 g
Couscous, uncooked	180 g	135 g	120 g	90 g	60 g	45 g	22 g
Oats, uncooked quick	90 g	65 g	60 g	45 g	30 g	22 g	11 g
Table salt	300 g	230 g	200 g	150 g	100 g	75 g	40 g
Butter	240 g	180 g	160 g	120 g	80 g	60 g	30 g
Vegetable shortening	190 g	140 g	125 g	95 g	65 g	48 g	24 g
Chopped fruits and vegetables	150 g	110 g	100 g	75 g	50 g	40 g	20 g
Nuts, chopped	150 g	110 g	100 g	75 g	50 g	40 g	20 g
Nuts, ground	120 g	90 g	80 g	60 g	40 g	30 g	15 g
Bread crumbs, fresh, loosely packed	60 g	45 g	40 g	30 g	20 g	15 g	8 g

Liquid (Fluid or Volume) Measurements (approximate):			
1 teaspoon		1/3 tablespoon	5 ml
1 tablespoon	1/2 fluid ounce	3 teaspoons	15 ml, 15 cc
2 tablespoons	1 fluid ounce	1/8 cup, 6 teaspoons	30 ml, 30 cc
1/4 cup	2 fluid ounces	4 tablespoons	59 ml
1/3 cup	2 2/3 fluid ounces	5 tablespoons + 1 teaspoon	79 ml
1/2 cup	4 fluid ounces	8 tablespoons	118 ml
2/3 cup	5 1/3 fluid ounces	10 tablespoons + 2 teaspoons	158 ml
3/4 cup	6 fluid ounces	12 tablespoons	177 ml
7/8 cup	7 fluid ounces	14 tablespoons	207 ml
1 cup	8 fluid ounces/ 1/2 pint	16 tablespoons	237 ml
2 cups	16 fluid ounces/ 1 pint	32 tablespoons	473 ml
4 cups	32 fluid ounces	1 quart	946 ml
1 pint	16 fluid ounces/ 1 pint	32 tablespoons	473 ml
2 pints	32 fluid ounces	1 quart	946 ml, 0.946 liters
8 pints	1 gallon/ 128 fluid ounces		3785 ml, 3.78 liters
4 quarts	1 gallon/ 128 fluid ounces		3785 ml, 3.78 liters
1 liter	1.057 quarts		1000 ml
1 gallon	128 fluid ounces		3785 ml, 3.78 liters

Dry Weight Measurements

		Ounces	Pounds	Metric
1/16 teaspoon	a dash			
1/8 teaspoon or less	a pinch or 6 drops			.5 ml
1/4 teaspoon	15 drops			1 ml
1/2 teaspoon	30 drops			2 ml
1 teaspoon	1/3 tablespoon	1/6 ounce		5 ml
3 teaspoons	1 tablespoon	1/2 ounce		14 grams
1 tablespoon	3 teaspoons	1/2 ounce		14 grams
2 tablespoons	1/8 cup	1 ounce		28 grams
4 tablespoons	1/4 cup	2 ounces		56.7 grams
5 tablespoons plus 1 teaspoon	1/3 cup	2.6 ounces		75.6 grams
8 tablespoons	1/2 cup	4 ounces	1/4 pound	113.4 grams
10 tablespoons plus 2 teaspoons	2/3 cup	5.2 ounces		158 ml
12 tablespoons	3/4 cup	6 ounces	.375 pound	177 ml
16 tablespoons	1 cup	8 ounces	1/2 pound	225 ml
32 tablespoons	2 cups	16 ounces	1 pound	450 ml
64 tablespoons	4 cups or 1 quart	32 ounces	2 pounds	907 ml

Pectin Guide

Pectin levels in fruit is very important when making any jam, preserves, jellies and for some chutneys. The lower the pectin, the less likely you're going to be able to achieve a good "set" on your final product. This can be easily corrected by checking the levels of pectin in your main ingredients. You could combine fruits with low to high pectin levels. Another popular method is to use "jam sugar" which has additional pectin added. The final method can be to add lemon juice, as citrus fruit has higher levels and the juice will give some of the additional pectin required. A good rule of thumb for pectin is based on whether the fruit as seeds within the fruit, on the outside of the fruit or on the outside. Fruits such as blackberries and strawberries tend to have low pectin levels. These are the fruits with the seeds on the outside. Conversely, fruits such as apples, oranges and lemons have seeds or pips on the inside and are higher in pectin. Although technically not a fruit, but used as a fruit, rhubarb has no seeds and is also a low pectin ingredient. As with everything though, there are always exceptions to the rule!

High	Medium	Low
Apple	Apricots	Cherries
Blackcurrants	Blackberries	Elderberries
Cranberries	Greengages	Figs
Damsons	Loganberries	Medlars
Gooseberries	Peaches	Mulberries
Lemons	Plums (generally)	Pears
Acid Plums	Raspberries	Rhubarb
Quinces		Strawberries
Redcurrants		

Contributor's List

Zoe Ayling
Stephen Baird
Penny Baxter
Suzan Brett
Vanessa Brett Davey
Ann Brooks
Alison Bull
Auntie Win From NZ
Jean Baker
Jenny Blake
Jacqui Bones
Valerie Callen
Sue Chambers
Phillipa Clarke
Tracey Colley
Alice Duckworth
Lou Duggan
Cid Eric
Ben Ferrier
Ali Fisher
Janet Ford
Linda Ford
Mary Fothergill
Natasha Garner
Kate Gibbs
Janet Gibson
Helen Godfrey
Tracy Goree
Finn Hannard
Jayne Hickling
Midge Holdsworth
Jackie Hughes
Helen Hunter
Sue Imrie
Lisa Johnston
Ieva Knell
Micheala Knight
Valentyna Kryvokon
Cara Kussan
Rachel Laing
Pauline Lord
Devina Lynn
Moi MacMillan
Ann Marie
Nikki Mason
Christina Mell
Steven Moseley
Chris Murray
Karen Parry

Amy Patrick
Lesley Peachey
Jackie Peat
Anna Penelope
Caroline Perley (via Carla Boyd)
Linda Phillips
Alec Popkin
Sue Popkin
Merle Prewett
Lesley Rayner
Julie Reppe
Alison Renshaw
Nan Roberts Massey
Sharon Roberts Ramones
Anne Robinson
Anne Roseveare
Helen Ruffles
Jane Scrivens
Steven Sehmbi
Patricia Serrell
Kayleigh Shaw
Lynda Smith
Celia Stapleton
Jennifer Stead
Jean Stiff
Brian Sturrock
Caz Sumner
Bev Toogood
Hazel Turner
Alex Vogler-El Masri
Katrina Watson
Debs Webster
Kelly Webster
Heidi Whyley
Lynda Williams
Sarah Williams
Rebecca Willmott
Teresa Witham
Anne Wriglesworth
Kate Wood
Ham Yam
Gillian Young
Hazel Young

Image Only Contributed by:
Mandy Bellis
Alma Crosby
Elaine Kelleher
Ann Morris
Naomi Pickard
Karen Synnuck
Amanda Whatley
Additional Images by: Vanessa Brett Davey

Index

Nanny Cakes by Sarah Godfrey.

Short Crust Pastry
2oz Margarine
2oz Caster Sugar
1 Egg
2oz Self raising flour
Raspberry Jam

Technically Maid's of Honour- but I renamed them Nanny Cakes when I was very little. Heat the oven to 180c. Make up the short crust pastry (½ fat to flour). Roll this out and cut into circles using a scone cutter. Grease and flour the pans of a cupcake/ fairy cake tin. The cutter needs to be big enough to create a circle which will coat the inside of the small cake tin. No need to blind bake. Make up the sponge cake mixture and put to the side. Put a teaspoon of raspberry (or any jam that you have to hand) in the bottom of each pastry case. Next, put a teaspoon of the cake mix on top of the jam, inside the pastry cases.

Put the cakes in the oven for around 20 minutes, or until the sponge cake springs back. Remove from the oven and allow to cool slightly before removing from the tins and cooling on a cooling rack. Love and enjoy xxxx

Printed in Great Britain
by Amazon